Brazelton Way

also by T. Berry Brazelton, M.D.

SLEEP
The
Brazelton Way

T. Berry Brazelton, M.D.
Joshua D. Sparrow, M.D.

A Merloyd Lawrence Book
PERSEUS PUBLISHING
A Member of the Perseus Books Group

PHOTO CREDITS

**Photographs on page 50 and title page [lower right]
by Janice Fullman**

Photograph on page xiv by Dorothy Littell Greco

**Photographs on page 6 and title page [upper and lower left,
upper right] by Marilyn Nolt**

Many of the designations used by manufacturers and sellers to distinguish
their products are claimed as trademarks. Where those designations appear
in this book and Perseus Publishing was aware of a trademark claim, the designations have been printed in initial capital letters.

Library of Congress Control Number: 2002114466
ISBN 0-7382-0782-9

Perseus Publishing is a Member of the Perseus Books Group.
Find us on the World Wide Web at http://www.perseuspublishing.com

Perseus Publishing books are available at special discounts for bulk purchases
in the U.S. by corporations, institutions, and other organizations. For more
information, please contact the Special Markets Department at the Perseus
Books Group, 11 Cambridge Center, Cambridge, MA 02142, or call (800)
255-1514 or (617) 252-5298, or e-mail j.mccrary@perseusbooks.com.

Text design by Trish Wilkinson
Set in 11-point AGaramond by the Perseus Books Group

First printing, January 2003
1 2 3 4 5 6 7 8 9 10—06 05 04 03

To the children and parents who have
taught us so much through the years

Contents

Preface

Ever since the first *Touchpoints* book was published in 1992, I have been asked by parents and professionals all over the country to write some short, practical books about the common challenges that parents face as they raise their children. Among the most common are crying, discipline, and getting a baby or child to sleep, topics that we address in this Brazelton Way series.

In my years of pediatric practice, families have taught me that problems in these areas often arise predictably as a child develops. In these short books I have tried to address the problems with crying, discipline, and sleep that parents are bound to encounter as their children regress just before they make their next developmental leap. Each book describes these "touchpoints" of crying, discipline, or sleep, so that parents can better understand their child's behavior. Each also offers practical suggestions on how parents can help children master the particular challenges they face in these areas and get back on track.

As with *Touchpoints Three to Six*, I have invited Joshua Sparrow, M.D., to co-author these books with me, to add his perspective as a child psychiatrist. In general, these books focus on the concerns and opportunities of the first six years of life, though occasionally we refer to older children's issues. In a final chapter of each book, special problems are discussed, though these short books are not intended to cover these topics exhaustively, nor are they meant to replace firsthand professional diagnosis and treatment. Instead, we hope that these books will serve as easy-to-use guides for parents to turn to as they face their child's growing pains, or the "touchpoints" that signal exciting leaps of development.

Though difficulties such as "colic" or excessive crying, middle of the night wakings, or temper tantrums, for example, are both common and predictable, they make great demands on parents. These kinds of problems are for the most part temporary and not serious. Yet without support and understanding, a family can be overwhelmed, and a child's development can veer seriously off course. It is our hope that the straightforward information provided in these books will help prevent those unnecessary derailments and provide reassurance for parents in times of uncertainty, so that even in those challenging moments, the excitement and joy of helping a young child grow can be rekindled.

SLEEP
The *Brazelton Way*

CHAPTER 1

Sleeping Through the Night

As I speak to parents around the country, I am most often asked about sleep: "How can I get my baby to sleep at night?" "How can I help him sleep through? When he awakens, I do too, and I can't get back to sleep." "Should I sleep with him? If I do, how will I get him out of my bed later?" Parents deserve answers as they face these years when sleep is their most pressing concern.

Both parents and babies need sleep. But their needs are very different. Before becoming parents, most people take sleeping through the night for granted. Then, suddenly, this is no longer possible. "I haven't slept a full night since my baby was born" is the most common complaint of new parents. Sleep-deprived adults long for their lost 8-hour stretches of sleep.

For parent and child to fit into each other's lives, the baby must learn to share the rhythms of sleep and waking on which family day and night rhythms are based.

A baby's sleep is different from adult sleep. Sleep is essential to his development, but sleep itself is also developing as a baby grows. A great deal is accomplished in sleep, such as brain and bodily growth, even preparation for the next day's learning, remembering, and paying attention.

For the baby, learning to sleep is part of becoming independent. For a parent, teaching a child to sleep means being able to separate, and to step back and allow the baby to "learn" to be independent at night.

Many pressures on parents make it difficult to set up consistent patterns of sleep. Parents who are away all day at work find it almost impossible to leave their babies at night. "Every time he rolls over or cries out at night, I feel that I have to go to him. I haven't had enough time with him during the day. Why can't I make up for it by sleeping with him at night?" Without realizing it, hard-working parents often interfere with their child's sleep patterns at night. For many, it's their only chance to be together.

For parents who have had any major worries about their baby, leaving that baby to learn to sleep can become a harrowing ordeal. "Will he stop breathing in the middle of the night? His breathing gets so irregular when he's sleeping." Even when such fears are unfounded, learning when to go to a baby at night and how to help him get to sleep by himself are rarely easy.

One of the biggest challenges a new parent faces is learning to live with sleeplessness. The feeling of responsibility for this precious new bundle adds to a new parent's difficulty in falling back to sleep. No one can ever be prepared for the physical demands of waking every few hours through the night. But it will pass! Eventually. As a baby grows, the way he sleeps changes. The first few months are the hardest. Patience and hope can help. During the early months, first-time parents may find it hard to believe that some parents actually choose to have more children, knowing that they will face those sleepless nights all over again. But later, parents even look back with longing on these night-time opportunities for warm, cozy cuddling.

Understanding a baby's sleep patterns will be a step toward establishing a smooth nightly routine. As your baby learns to sleep, you'll learn how to respond when you hear your baby wake up at night, when to soothe your baby, when to expect he'll fall right back to sleep, and when your baby needs you to encourage him to set-tle himself.

This is more complicated than it seems. A child who had been sleeping on his own at one point in time will later go through periods when he needs more help. We call these moments "touchpoints," times when a new step ahead is to be taken—at a cost. These are special times when a baby's efforts to learn a new skill (such as pulling to stand, or walking) seem to interfere with ear-lier accomplishments, such as sleeping through the night. Parents don't expect these disruptive sleep periods. Understanding them may give parents a better chance to offer their baby reassurance and limits. He will need these to learn how to get himself back to sleep. Learning to sleep is a necessary step toward independence.

One of the greatest rewards of being a parent is to slip into the child's room and to see the cozy, delicious look of a safely sleeping child—the regular breathing, the smell, the soft skin, the curly hair. My daughter always slept with the palms of her hands pressed together under her cheek, as if she were praying.

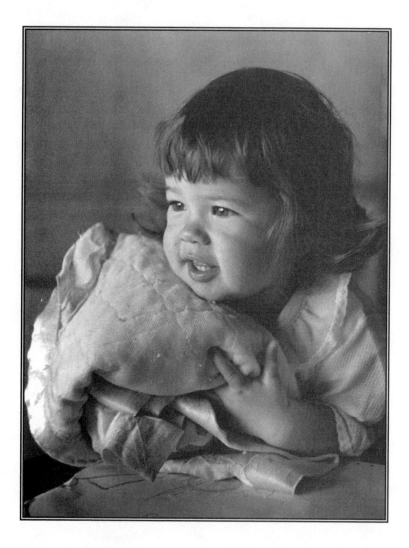

CHAPTER 2

The Touchpoints of Sleep

Sleep Before Birth

It is reassuring to remember that a newborn infant has already had many months to adapt to a mother's pattern of sleeping and waking. The mother, too, has become aware of her baby-to-be's sleep-wake cycles.

By 6 or 7 months of pregnancy, a mother already knows when and under what conditions she will feel activity and kicking. She also knows that if she doesn't eat on time, or if she is stressed or tired, these very active periods may be delayed. Most mothers expect the kicking activity at the end of the day, when they are tired and ready to lie down to rest. Often they may say, "That's the only time I can notice the swimming around—I'm too busy otherwise." Some experts believe this cycling of activity is linked to low blood sugar, or to lactic acid, which goes up when a mother is weary.

The unborn baby is already adjusting to the mother's day and night cycle. Behaving differently in her own cycles of alert and inactive states, the unborn baby is "learning" to adjust to her environment. Mothers have told me that the sleep–wake cycles became longer and more predictable as their pregnancy passed into the eighth and ninth months.

To learn more about these patterns, which mothers have long known, my colleagues and I tried some exciting experiments with 7-month-old fetuses. We used ultrasound machines to watch their responses to sounds and lights outside their mothers' bellies:

- First we set off a loud buzzer. After the first buzz, the fetus startled. The startles decreased with each buzz, and disappeared by the fifth or sixth time. The fetus seemed to have screened out the disturbing noise. We saw the fetus stop moving, bring hand to mouth, and turn away from the direction of the sound.

- When we rattled a soft rattle the fetus turned toward the rattle. From this we learned that even before birth, a baby can shut out disturbing noises, and respond to more attractive ones.

- With bright light, we demonstrated the same effect. The fetus startled at the first flash, but by the fourth no longer responded, and turned away. When we shone a pinpoint light on the mother's belly, the fetus turned toward it. The powerful operating room light was overwhelming for the fetus, whereas the pinpoint light seemed interesting.

When we describe these experiments to parents, they are fascinated and relieved to know that their tiny newborns have arrived with the ability to handle noise and bright light, and to adapt to their new world. Before birth, babies learn to adapt their sleep–wake cycles to the parents' day–night cycle. They are preparing to fit into the outside environment even before delivery.

Newborn Sleep

Despite this preparation before birth, a newborn's sleep patterns are usually all over the map. The baby must recover from the disruption of labor and birth before she can reestablish a pattern to her sleep–wake cycle. She will though, but her sleep–wake cycle is changing anyway, as her brain matures. Her new surroundings are full of lights and noises. She is no longer in the warm protection of the womb. Sudden motions of her own arms and legs, called "startles," set off crying, which leads to helpless disorganization in the newborn baby—and, often, in the new parent. Soon though she will adapt her own sleep–wake cycles to those of her parents, though it may not seem soon enough.

Newborn Sleep and Temperament

The baby's temperament shapes her patterns of sleeping and waking from the start. Although the newborn is so disorganized and affected by the events of labor, delivery, and any medication given to the mother that her style or temperament is hard to predict, there are signs even in these early days.

We used to believe that newborn babies were alike, ready to be changed by those who cared for them. Any difficult behavior that arose was assumed to be the parents' fault. We were barely aware of the influence of medication or stressful events to which the mother had been exposed while carrying the baby. Nowadays, however, we know a lot about the wonderful, complex behavior of the newborn and how it can differ from baby to baby. We also know how these differences change the ways eager parents react to their newborns. In my first book, *Infants and Mothers,* I wrote of three different kinds of newborns: quiet, active, and "average." Together with others, I pointed out how important it is to "understand" these different babies and how they shape the world around them. Parents of course were already aware of these differences, but their observations were not always respected by experts.

In the years that followed, I designed a newborn evaluation that can be shared with new, passionate parents. Many parents are now familiar with this test, called the Newborn Behavioral Assessment Scale (NBAS), which is used at many hospitals after birth. We learned that to identify a newborn's abilities we had to work with a baby's temperament and sleep-wake states.

Newborn Sleep–Wake Cycles

The newborn has six easily identified sleep–wake states. These are: deep sleep, light sleep (or "rapid eye movement," REM), a drowsy state between sleep and awake, wide-awake alert, fussiness, and crying. In the first and the last states the baby shuts out stimulation from her surroundings. The others are transitional and the peak is the alert state. One of the most remarkable observations of the newborn baby is that she can actively maintain the alert state and the shut-out states of sleep and crying. She uses all her resources, her heart rate and breathing, the movements of her body, in her attempts to control interruptions to these states. In order to maintain the balance of her immature nervous system, she tries not to allow stimulation to overwhelm her. Soon after birth, she learns to cycle from sleep to awake to sleep to protect herself from too much stimulation, and to seek out the stimulation she needs. Awake and sleep states balance each other.

After a period of recovery from the overwhelming stimuli of birth and the new environment, the baby can cycle into an alert state in which she opens up to her new world. In that state, the responses of a newborn are amazing. Not only can she see and hear, but she can maintain her alert state—suppressing reflexes and motions in order to respond. She can make choices about what she does or doesn't want to respond to. And, if the activity around her is too overwhelming or too boring, she can slip into what appears to be a sleep state. This sleep state is almost like deep sleep because in this state she breathes deeply and regularly, has tightly closed eyes, and a rigidly controlled body. When the overstimulation ceases, a newborn will often wake up. This shows the baby's ability to protect herself with a sleep state. We call it "habituation"—the baby's way of shutting out the world around her.

Premature Infants' Sleep

Even in premature babies we see those 6 states and their attempts to manage them. A baby born before 30–32 weeks of pregnancy will not cycle predictably through sleep–wake states. After 32 weeks there is predictable cycling of active and inactive states. After 34 weeks, the quiet intervals of rest between jumpy active states begin to lengthen. The bright lights and constant noise of the premature nursery can interfere with this. In our work with these "preemies" we didn't see these cycles until we made changes in the nursery. We began covering the incubators for at least an hour between the feedings at 3-hour intervals and did not allow tests or procedures to be done during these regular, protected hours. Then, the 35-week infants began to adapt to longer cycles of rest and activity. Feeding cycles also became more predictable. Since that time, premature nurseries have adopted some of these measures and parents have welcomed these signs of a predictable routine in their tiny, premature babies. Fragile babies needed protection to learn how to cycle through these states. It was critical to their recovery and their growth.

Soothing and Sleep

The ability to sleep and stay asleep is already an advantage, even in the newborn period. This will be more likely for a baby who can shut out outside disturbances and who can get her hand up to her mouth to suck and soothe.

Parents whose baby adapts easily by using her own abilities to self-soothe and be soothed are fortunate. Their baby's cycles of light and deep sleep, waking, feeding, and descent into sleep again may come easily, and by 4 weeks the cycles may fit into a 3- or 4-hour pattern that adapts to parents' days and nights. An active, vigorously responsive baby may be at the other end of the scale. She may be difficult to soothe and easy to rouse, and she may find it difficult to pay attention. These infants can be "taught" over time to control these states, but this can mean a longer, more difficult adjustment for parents.

Soothing an Active Baby

An active, easily disturbed baby often has difficulty finding her thumb or a comforting position. As she awakens and fusses, she startles. The startles set off crying and uncontrolled activity. The activity sets off more startles. A vicious cycle of activity and crying is set in motion. Parents

Ways to Help a Baby Calm Herself

- Swaddling half the body—the lower half.
- Helping her to find her thumb or her fist—to teach her hand-to-mouth maneuvers.
- Offering a pacifier for sucking.
- Rocking her and singing to her.
- Carrying the baby on the mother's (or father's) chest.
- Quietly putting the baby down, singing to her.
- Using a continuous sound, such as the noise of a washing machine.
- Sleeping her on her back, but slightly propped at a small angle to one side to cut down on startles.

are driven to pick the baby up, to bounce her up and down, to swaddle her, to try all sorts of remedies, even placing the baby seat on the washing machine, or driving over rough roads. The baby's frantic activity is matched by her parents! But as soon as the parents' efforts stop, the baby is likely to rouse again, more worn out than before. Already, temperament is beginning to play an important role for parents and infant.

Active, easily stimulated babies can also be fed more often to try to soothe them. They may cry and gulp air down so that they need more frequent burping. It is important not to overstimulate such babies. Think of them as having a sensitive, easily overloaded nervous system. Creating a soothing, quiet environment can be a help. It is difficult for a parent not to feel like a failure with a baby who wakens and cries every hour or so and who is so difficult to soothe.

Gradually, however, parents can learn what works and will feel less helpless. Very sensitive, easily roused babies are often as challenging as active babies. The suggestions we have outlined above are also useful for these babies.

A baby needs up to 16 hours of sleep a day, but only half of it may occur at night when parents can catch up on their sleep. As we will see in the following sections, there are many strategies for parents to use to help their baby work toward night sleeping and day waking.

Sleep Position for All Babies
The American Academy of Pediatrics has recommended that infants be placed on their backs for sleeping, to reduce the incidence of Sudden Infant Death Syndrome (SIDS). Extensive studies have shown that the incidence of SIDS is reduced when infants sleep on their backs. A national campaign called "Back to Sleep" has promoted this important issue.

In order to get infants used to back sleeping, it must be started from the first. Some infants seem to prefer stomach sleeping, for it helps to keep their arms and legs still whenever they startle. This makes the startles, which are often a normal part of every light sleep cycle, less likely to disturb their sleep. These babies may have difficulty comforting themselves on their backs. Though settling babies for sleep on their backs can make life more difficult for parents, it does help prevent SIDS, so even parents of active, light-sleeping babies will want to try to follow this advice.

Keeping a baby's hands uncovered can help her learn to suck her fingers for comfort while sleeping on her back. Also, swaddling babies firmly from the waist down can reduce the cycling of startles and waking. When babies sleep on their backs, they need to play on their bellies during the day. This is important so that their back muscles will develop well. (See also *Sudden Infant Death Syndrome* and *Safety in Sleep* in Chapter 3.)

3 Weeks

By the third week, the cycles of sleep and waking may begin to become more organized. Feedings are more successful, and parents are getting to know their baby. At first the mother's milk or the bottle may have been necessary every 1 to 2 hours. But gradually a parent begins to take control—to urge the baby to stretch out the feedings. Often this is unconscious and can be as simple as waiting a few minutes before rushing to feed the baby. The restlessness and the fussing that were taken so seriously at first are seen now as "just waking up." In this way, the cycles become stretched out to 3-hour cycles. The baby's alertness is prolonged in the middle of the cycle, just as longer sleep periods balance it at each end of the cycle. As parents become more certain of the baby's cues, they recognize the difference between the fussy cry of waking up or of boredom from that of a hungry cry.

End-of-the-Day Fussing

At about 3 weeks, a fussy period at the end of the day is likely to begin. Mothers have told me that they can predict this fussy or irritable crying period because their baby begins to be jumpy, easily overstimulated, and often inconsolable. Mothers also tell me that after the fussing is over, their babies sleep better. After a parent makes sure that it's not hunger, discomfort, or pain, the baby may need to cry for 5–10 minutes at a time to discharge an immature, overloaded nervous system. After a period of this fussing, followed by frequent soothing and burping, the baby is likely to settle down to quiet, regular sleep. It is as if she were finally exhausted and had discharged her overloaded nervous energy. This ability to sleep afterward makes the fussy period worth it.

Day and Night

Many newborns seem to reverse day and night. According to parents, they sleep all day. Are they protecting themselves from noisy, overstimulating environments? This can make them wake up and fuss during the parents' nighttime sleep hours. What can a sleep-deprived adult do about this? I have often recommended that the parent begin by waking the baby an hour before her usual late morning wakening. Stimulate her to stay awake. Every 3 or 4 days, pull her back another hour until all her activity and alert states are occurring in the early evening. After that, the baby may begin to stretch out her sleeping periods at night.

Parents will be reassured when they recognize that their baby's sleep, which at first seemed to be totally unpredictable, is beginning to fall into a pattern. Arthur H. Parmelee, M.D., charted the waking hours of a number of babies at 1–4 weeks (unpredictable) and 12–16 weeks (clear pattern) and made the following graphs.

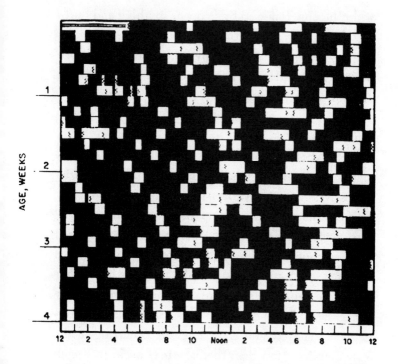

A typical pattern of waking hours (shown in white) for babies
from birth to 4 weeks. Graph courtesy of Arthur H. Parmelee
Jr., M.D.

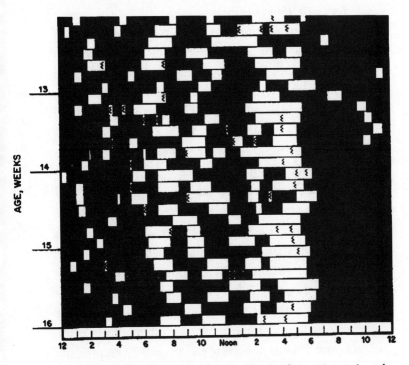

Waking hours (shown in white) of babies from 12 to 16 weeks. Graph courtesy of Arthur H. Parmelee Jr., M.D.

Co-sleeping: The Family Bed

Sleep-deprived new parents often take the infant into their own bed. The warm presence of their bodies can soothe the infant. It works, so why not? Because a child who sleeps with her parents as a baby and toddler is unlikely to learn how to get herself to sleep and stay asleep, she will have trouble giving this up for her own bed when her parents are ready. Parents will find it useful to think this issue over from the start.

Our mainstream culture insists on independence as a value more than do many others. We start early with our expectation that babies must be unswaddled during the day, and sleep alone in their cribs at night. We are asking a lot of our most immature members to become independent and resourceful as early as we do.

Mothers in the United States who co-sleep talk about the ease of breastfeeding when the infant rouses every 3–4 hours. Parents also value the rewards of keeping the baby with them after being away at work all day. Separation at night can seem very painful. Of course, parents realize when they begin co-sleeping that the separation is only delayed and will become necessary later on. By the second or third year, the child will have learned to depend on the parents' presence to help her get back down to sleep from brief awakenings from light sleep or deep sleep. Then it will be far more difficult for her to learn to put herself to sleep and to stay asleep through the light-deep sleep cycles. Parents must weigh these decisions to suit their own lives, the traditions of their culture, and the needs of their individual baby.

Studies about co-sleeping to prevent SIDS have been contradictory: Some say that co-sleeping may prevent SIDS, others say that it won't. In 1997, the American Academy of Pediatrics took the position that co-sleeping did not prevent SIDS. In 2001, the U.S. Consumer Product Safety Commission (CPSC) and the Juvenile Products Manufacturers Association (JPMA) reported that 180 children (mostly under 1 year) placed in adult beds had died in the preceding two years. The CPSC recommends that babies not be placed in adult beds. But the jury may be out until we learn more. Did any of these infants have other conditions that could cause sudden death? How safe were the beds they slept in? All the advice about avoiding soft bedding and pillows, or toys that could suffocate a baby in the crib, also apply to co-sleeping. (See also *Co-sleeping* in Chapter 3.)

Helping Your Child Learn to Get Back to Sleep
In order to sleep through the night, a child must "learn" to reorganize herself after the cycle of deep sleep and

waking every 3–4 hours. A baby must be able to come up to light sleep, cry out, scrabble around in bed, comfort herself, and get back down into deep sleep. This is a tall order, and it takes time. During an 8-hour period of sleep, it is normal for a baby to become wakeful and restless at least twice; in 12 hours of sleep, at least three times. To sleep through the night, she must learn to get through these times on her own.

Parents who feel the need to go to her at each rousing will inevitably become part of her pattern of settling back down. If they pick her up to feed or play with her, if they rock her back to sleep in their arms, they will become part of the child's self-comforting habits. To lead the child toward comforting herself, parents can comfort a child to the point of a drowsy state—by rocking, singing softly, or reading to her. When she is drowsy, *but not yet asleep,* place her in her crib. There, sit beside her to pat her, and to croon, "You can get yourself down. You can get yourself down. You can do it. You can do it." As she finally gets herself into a self-soothing ritual— sucking her thumb, curling up, fingering her blanket or a favorite stuffed animal (what we call a "lovey")—she will begin to feel competent and able to comfort herself at each waking. Gradually, the parent will need to do less and less, so that the baby can take over.

This accomplishment demands at least three things:

- the parents' determination that the baby will learn to soothe herself;
- the baby's ability to stretch out to a 3- or 4-hour pattern without hunger interfering; and
- that the baby's nervous system is mature enough to allow her to stretch out sleeping periods through the night and to find a self-soothing pattern for herself. It seems that this often becomes possible by 4 months of age.

Recognizing a Baby's Needs

In the first few weeks, I would recommend that new parents feed their infant whenever the infant appears hungry (feeding her on demand), as a way of getting to know their newborn. Each time parents try to feed a crying baby, the infant will let them know whether she is crying out of hunger. As parents try other techniques—holding, rocking, singing—they will begin to match their responses to the baby's needs. They will recognize different cries: hunger, boredom, fatigue, discomfort, pain, discharging an overloaded nervous system. As the infant begins to form patterns of waking and sleeping, parents can begin to respond to these and help her remain alert and responsive in the daylight hours. As they learn to understand and respond to their infant's behavior, parents automatically push a small infant to stretch out between feedings. Watch for the balance of awake and sleep states. It will help you understand how to help her into a reliable sleep pattern.

Starting a Bedtime Ritual

As the sleeping pattern becomes more reliable over the next few weeks, it is time to begin to establish bedtime rituals that will be useful throughout the child's infancy.

- Nurse the baby or bottle-feed her in your arms.
- Rock and sing.
- Calm her and then place her in her crib *before* she is asleep. If necessary, rouse her to a semi-awake state before putting her to bed—so that she can learn to put *herself* to sleep.
- Sit beside her to croon and pat her down.
- *Never* prop a bottle in bed beside her. She could choke and inhale milk into her lungs. Milk or even sugar water or juice in her mouth all night can harm her future teeth, so don't leave her with a bottle.

4 Months

By 4 months of age, the baby's nervous system will have matured enough so that she is able to sleep 8 hours without a feeding or other attention from parents (though still she may not). This process is helped along because parents will have been unconsciously pushing the baby to stretch out her feeding pattern during the day.

While babies differ considerably in their need for sleep, between 4 to 6 months they may be sleeping roughly 10 or 11 hours at night, with one or two wakings. During the day they will sleep another 4 or 5 hours over the course of two or three naps. (See the waking–sleeping graphs earlier in this chapter.)

Stretching Out the Waking Hours

You can help your baby learn to sleep longer at night by stretching out her waking hours during the day. At 4 months, babies love to be talked to. They will lie in a crib or in a reclining chair and gurgle back and forth with an adult for 15 to 20 minutes without a break. When they are being changed, they start the cycle of gurgling and talking. Arms up, face brightening, they coo and gurgle. Each change can be a prolonged game.

Feedings, too, become exciting. A baby will stop sucking to look up at her parent expectantly, as if hoping the parent will look down to talk, to stroke her cheek, to tickle her feet as she waves them in the air.

When a baby starts to fuss between feedings a mobile can be moved over her to focus her attention for the next 15 minutes. As one-armed reaching begins to develop, a string of reachable, touchable toys can absorb her interest. (These will need to be removed when she's older, more active, and at risk of dangerously tangling herself up in the strings.) The baby is becoming involved in the world around her. Parents can rely on this widening interest to help a baby stretch out 2½- to 3-hour awake periods between feedings during the day to 3½- to 4-hour intervals. At the same time as this or because of it, her ability to stretch out her sleep at night will develop as well.

All of a sudden, parents realize that their baby is sleeping from 6 P.M. straight through to the 10 P.M. feeding. Often a baby will wake at 2 A.M., scriggle around in bed, and let out a few rousing shrieks. Parents then rush in to see what has made her so upset. They may find her lying wide-eyed in her crib, sucking on her fist, fingering the satin on her blanket, looking out at them expectantly. If they feed her, they may find that their every-4-hour day is off to a 2 A.M. start.

A Bedtime Ritual at 4 Months

- Parents can take turns.
- Read from a small, simple book, pointing to the pictures.
- Tickle the baby's toes, pat her cheek, play with her hair.
- Then a feeding.
- Try a rocking chair.
- If the baby falls asleep during the feeding, rouse her to a semi-awake state. Put her in her crib half-awake.
- Position her on her back so that she can reach her thumb.
- As the baby falls asleep, her thumb in her mouth, her hand may finger her sleeper or the top of her blanket.
- As she falls into deeper sleep, her sucking will soften in sound, coming in bursts of sucks, then none.
- Creep out of the room and enjoy the peace!

If, instead, parents wait for a few moments, the baby may be able to find her thumb, her blanket, her "lovey," and to comfort herself back down into sleep again. If they hover they will interrupt this cycle. Had they rushed to feed her every 3 hours in the day, she might not have learned to stretch out at night. Now, parents have another decision to make. If they go to her to awaken and feed her at 10 P.M., before they go to bed, she may stretch out from 10 P.M. to 6 A.M., giving them this 8-hour interval for their own sleep. I have always recommended this when an initial 8-hour stretch (often from 6 P.M. to 2 A.M.) is already firmly in place. If they can rouse the baby and play with her briefly, rock and sing to her in a bedtime routine, she is likely to be able to stretch out her sleep afterward. She is likely to rouse herself less violently at 2 A.M. and to get herself back down to sleep.

Toward Independent Sleeping

If a parent encourages an infant to rely on her own resources during the day and night, and avoids rushing to her to pick her up and to feed her every time she cries out and scrabbles around in bed, the baby is likely to learn nighttime independence. It seems as if "learning" to sleep depends on learning to be independently resourceful. Some babies, who are easily excited and who lose control in startles that rouse them, may not be able to settle themselves. But most babies can learn to comfort themselves by this age.

Parents often ask whether this means letting a baby "cry it out." I explain that this does not mean deserting the baby at night. Parents can go to the baby, sit quietly beside her, pat her down gently. I often recommend that a parent sing a quiet song as they pat, "You can do it!

You can do it! You can do it yourself!" Don't respond to her invitations for other more lively interactions. Keep her focused on her job—settling herself down to sleep. By not taking her out to feed her or play with her, you are encouraging her to rely on her own pattern of self-comforting. This may be expecting independence before some active, hypersensitive babies are ready for it. But most 4-month-old babies are ready. On the other hand, parents who have been away from home all day may not be ready for such a separation. They may need these periods of closeness at night as times of reunion at the end of a hectic day.

Sleep-Wake Cycles from Childcare to Home

When a working parent arrives to pick up the baby at the end of a long day, the baby is likely to fall apart. This can be very upsetting to parents. But it is a sign that she's missed you all day and wants *your* cuddling. When you have calmed her, it's time to play with her. Feed her when she tires. After an exciting time with you in the evening, she is likely to be ready for the bedtime ritual and for sleep.

When a baby is in childcare, I always recommend that the caregiver provide a long afternoon nap or quiet time so that the baby can be prepared to be alert and playful when the parent is available. But if a baby sleeps later than 4 P.M., she will be up and awake until 10 P.M. and is less likely to stretch out to 8 hours of sleep afterward. The baby's internal clock may not get adjusted to a day-night cycle of sleeping when her parents are asleep.

The 4-Month Touchpoint and Sleep

After 4 months, a "touchpoint" (see my book *Touchpoints*) is around the corner. Along with a burst in learning, a baby tends to fall apart—both night and day. She will be unpredictable and disorganized. The rhythmic sleep-wake pattern will suffer and she'll begin to wake more easily again. Her senses are sharper now, and she is able to take in much more information about her world.

For example, now she can focus not only on the nearby face of the parent who is feeding her, but also on objects on the other side of the room. Her new excitement about the sights and sounds all around her means that she's bound to lose interest quickly in feeding, and she won't stay at the breast or bottle. She is likely to start out hungrily, suck–suck–suck–suck. But, then, the infant notices a new noise—a plane out the window—or a sudden interesting sight—the pattern of light the sun makes on the wall. She won't suck. She pulls away to look and listen. Every feeding gets interrupted, unless

Helping a 4-Month-Old to Sleep

- Realize that this is a touchpoint—a backward step that goes with new spurts in her ability to use her body and her mind. The regression won't last more than a week or two unless it is reinforced.
- Don't pick her up or feed her. If you really aren't sure whether she is waking because she is hungry or teething, wake her at 10 P.M. to feed her, rub her gums, and let her chew on her fingers to soothe her teeth. Then watch to see whether these maneuvers are the answer.
- If not, be prepared to keep her in her crib.
- At bedtime, reinforce the ritual of rocking, singing, reading to her, and giving her her "lovey"—a blanket, a stuffed animal, or her thumb.
- When she rouses, help her find her lovey. Encourage the thumb. Fall back on singing softly and patting her down. This is only a *temporary* backward slide. She is bound to be comforted by familiar old routines. "You can do it! You can do it! You can do it!" You are urging her to take over her own return to deep sleep.
- Gradually try to leave it to her. Wait a few minutes before you go to her. Call out softly to let her know you are there. If you do go to her, don't take her out of her bed. Remind her that she can put herself back down to sleep.
- Make her lovey important to her during the day—for example, when she's frustrated or hurt. Hand it to her and let her know that she can fall back on it. This may be difficult and may feel like deserting her, but it will help her become more independent. You are joining her in these new steps toward independence, and it may not be easy—for it may feel as if you're making your baby grow up too fast.

she's fed in a dark, quiet room. She would rather look around or listen to an interesting sound than eat. Of course, this alarms parents unless they understand her reason for refusing to feed.

A breastfeeding mother is bound to take it personally. "My milk is no good. Maybe she's teething and it hurts to suck." She may be teething, it's true. If so, wash your hands and then rub on her lower front gums where her first teeth will emerge. You will rub out the swelling and she will feel more comfortable sucking again. But she may not be teething. She may just be disorganized by her new interest in the world around her. She can get enough milk in a short time, but it takes much longer to satisfy her interest in everything else. Although she won't eat like she used to, she is probably getting enough if she continues to grow and gain weight.

This same interest in her world is likely to affect her sleeping patterns. As she rouses from deep sleep every few hours, she is no longer interested in getting herself back down. If she hears a noise, even a snoring or groaning from your bed, or a clanking radiator, she's awake. If she can see anything exciting—even a reflected light from the street—she will want to follow it. She is likely to rouse and regress into her old pattern of demanding a feeding every 3 to 4 hours all over again. This waking up isn't likely to last more than a week, however, if parents can fall back on their earlier patterns: waiting to see whether she can put herself back down to sleep, and if she can't, patting her down in bed without taking her out.

If this doesn't work, feed and settle her every 4 hours, but watch for this new interest to wane. Then, begin to rely on the "wait to see" approach. It is likely that after the week or so of excitement, she will be ready to fall back into the sleep pattern she's developed earlier—of rousing every 4 hours, but then comforting herself back down into deep sleep.

If she rouses at 2 A.M. after having slept straight through from 6 or 7 P.M., try waking and feeding her again at 10 P.M., to see whether she will go from 10 P.M. to 6 A.M. while you are sleeping. Break the cycle for her. It may work. After this rousing is over, she is likely to sleep through a 6- to 8-hour cycle. In fact, many babies begin to sleep even longer—10 to 12 hours. But a baby who sleeps 12 hours is not actually asleep the entire time. She must rouse from sleep a few times during the night, and then settle herself. She is becoming independent.

Solid Food and Sleep

Solid food may keep an infant satisfied for longer than milk feedings. At 5 months, a baby can digest more complex solid food. Many parents feel that solids like rice cereal at the evening feeding are likely to help an infant this age get through the night. But the 5-month-old will need to have already learned to be independent when she rouses. Otherwise, feedings alone will not make much difference in her sleep.

7 to 8 Months

By 6 months, babies are often already sleeping for 12 hours a night, waking only briefly a few times. Most are still napping morning and afternoon for an hour or two. But in the coming months, this progress may be thrown off by other new developments.

Creeping

The next peak of night waking is likely to occur along with two new developmental spurts. One is the motor skill of creeping—which opens up the baby's world. At first, she creeps backward and one can see by her frustrated, disappointed-looking face that she already has her own ideas about "getting there." She wants to go forward, to reach farther than her arms will reach. A whole new world seems almost available. With creeping, with an ability to master her body, sitting and turning from one side to another, turning over, a baby's world takes on new meaning. "I can get there and I want to." This will be her big interest even in the middle of the night as soon as she bobs up at the end of a cycle of light (or even deep) sleep. She will want to repeat the moves that she's been practicing all day. Of course her sleep is bound to be interrupted.

New Awareness

The second spurt is in her widening awareness of the world. She is beginning to vocalize as part of her reaching out for important people: "mama" when she's in trouble and "dada" when she wants to play. But she is also approaching the very important stage of stranger awareness. As she becomes aware of differences among people, she will show her new ability to differentiate her mother from her mother's sister, her father from her father's brother. This fine awareness accompanies a spurt in cognitive development. Being left by an important person will be even more frightening than before. Being alone or in the dark at night takes on new meaning.

When she rouses to light sleep at 10 P.M., 2 A.M., or 5 A.M., she will turn over, or scrabble her way into an uncomfortable corner of the bed. She will recognize the frustration of being alone in the dark as something to protest. Once again, she is likely to revert to awakening every 3 to 4 hours at night. Parents will feel that they've lost the game of "teaching her to sleep through." They will go to her, "Why are you waking up? Are you hungry all over again? Are you getting more teeth? Did something scare you?" Naturally, the confused parent will get her up to comfort her and to feed her. Just as naturally, the cycle of unwanted waking is reinforced.

After a few repetitions at night, the parent will begin to realize that this is no longer an isolated event—"We're at it again. What do we do now? Should we let her cry it out? She's too big and too smart to pat her down to sleep again like we did when she was little."

10 Months

For a baby this age, many new achievements make the day so exciting that giving in to sleep is a last resort. Crawling and exploring have reached a peak. Her pincer grasp (she's been working on using her thumb and forefinger together for the past few months) makes it possible for her to pick up everything to put in her mouth. She has found that she can get an immediate response from her parents if she goes toward the light plug, the

TV, or the stove. "No! Don't touch that!" If she persists, someone will come to remove her. She is learning to control her world. It is *so* exciting! Why would any child this age give in to sleep?

Then comes pulling up to stand. Clinging from one piece of furniture to the next, she can pull herself around the house. Now she can reach precious or dangerous objects on tables. Now she is likely to have adults hover nearby at all times. If she crawls up to the stairs and starts to climb, they are likely to be there to extract her from danger. And she knows it!

Although she may have gotten back into an 8- to 10-hour sleep pattern as before, all of her energy is now going into standing up, getting going, cruising on the side of her crib, and discovering her world. There is bound to be another peak in night waking now. When she awakens from deep sleep, she automatically pulls herself up by the side of the crib. Once awake she realizes that she's hanging on to the side of her crib. How to get down? She starts to whimper, then to cry out, to act helpless as she stands hanging on to her cribside.

Parents have often called me to ask how to handle this renewed waking pattern. "She gets up on the side of her crib and she can't get back down. I have to go to her—all over again." "Can she get back down in the daytime?" I ask. "Yes." "Well, isn't it interesting that she can't get back down at night? Maybe you have to teach her that she can. When you go to her, give her a little shove. She'll bend in the middle, and find out that she can get back down by herself. But you don't need to desert her. Sit by her bed to help her fall asleep afterward." After a few nights, the baby will have learned how to get herself back down to sleep. At first parents may feel they are being dismissive of the child's pleas. But this is a chance to turn the child back to her own resources. What could be more respectful? Watch her face as she realizes that she herself is mastering this new transition.

An active child may continue to be so intrigued with standing that she needs more comforting, but most children will begin to handle their sleep patterns again.

12 Months

By the time they are 1 year old, many children will be sleeping somewhere between 11 and 12 hours at night. Some children will still have both a morning and an afternoon nap, but most will give up the morning nap sometime during the second year.

With the excitement of walking alone, however, new sleeping issues are likely to arise. The new toddler finds she can explore her world much more completely. She can crawl up on tables. She can even climb up her crib-side. If she tries to get out, remove any crib bumpers and move the mattress to the lowest possible level. It may be time to add a safety-approved extension to the side of the crib. If she can still climb out, it is time to move her to a bed. Usually this will be at 3–4 years, but for a number of children, the time comes earlier. It is certainly likely to be necessary that you go to her more often. With her increased power to explore, the child is realizing that she can both leave her parents around the corner, but also remind them that she's out of sight. A cry for help produces results in a few seconds. It becomes thrilling to set up games of "rescue me" in order to interrupt her parents' concentration—on the phone, at the stove, or any other activity. "You'd better stay by my side. I can get into all kinds of trouble now," she seems to beckon.

Affirming Bedtime Rituals

Bedtime rituals begin to be tested. No longer is the baby ready to go down smoothly and easily. Calling a parent back can become a power play. The parent needs to set a limit on the "game" of being called back—without getting entangled in the struggle. Unless the bedtime ritual really works to help her settle, unless she has firmly learned to put herself down into deep sleep, every bedtime separation can become a tussle as the toddler tests to see whether her parents really mean it or not.

This is the time for parents to recognize how hard it is for a child to give up one activity for another, especially for sleep. To help, warn the child in advance: "This is the last book we are going to read. I know it's hard to stop. But when it's over, time for a lullaby and kiss good night. Then—lights out." A little later say, "Remember this is the last story. We only have three more pages to read. Time to get yourself ready to say goodnight." When parents are certain that testing must end, the child will know it and comply.

Changes in Routine

Whenever there's a change in the household routine, she'll start waking again. "We just went away for the weekend. She stayed with her grandmother whom she loves. But since we got back, she's been waking at 2 A.M. every night. She knows that I feel guilty about having left her. Do you think she's playing on that?" Yes, I do. Not in an angry or intentional way, but she may have feelings left over from your being away. I'd certainly go to her and comfort her to sleep. The fact that you are determined that she can do it can be reassuring to her. I think you'll find that when she does start sleeping through again, she'll be as happy as you are. A few weeks later I often hear: "I can't tell you how delighted she was the morning after the night she slept all the way through. She said 'I did it!' and hugged her blanket."

After a stressful experience, such as an appointment for immunizations, a toddler is almost bound to wake up at night. She may cry out as if she were terrified, though nightmares are more likely after age 2. As her push toward independence continues, her dependency may well show up at night. Reassure her but let her know you expect her to get herself back to sleep. During the day, you may need to allow her to be more dependent. Assure her that she's really doing a big girl's job by comforting herself with her thumb and her lovey. She may come to your bed more often after a stressful day. I'd see this as a plea for more comfort.

Prepare her each time for learning all over again how to return to her own sleep patterns. Reemphasize her lovey and her self-comforting pattern. The goal will be to help her remember that she can get herself back down. Your anger and frustration won't work. Sympathy and understanding will. But she'll also need your firm expectation that she will learn again to sleep through the night. When she does, she will be as relieved as you are.

2 to 3 Years

In the second and third years, a child will strive for independence by insisting on her own way. Parents will come to expect her to say, "No!" and "Let me do it myself!"

As the struggles of the second year surge, many toddlers will have night wakings. Parents will need to see these as temporary and to help their child to relearn to get herself to sleep all over again each time. There will be periods of resistance, of calling them to her. She will cry out as if in a bad dream. She will demand their presence as if each separation were a tragic one. When her parents are vulnerable, having been away all day, she will sense their vulnerability and demand their presence at night. It is up to parents to decide.

Night Terrors

Night terrors may begin in the second and third years. Sitting bolt upright in her bed, the child shrieks inconsolably, yet is not entirely awake. It may be difficult to rouse her, and she is likely to fall back to sleep before waking up. To see a child screaming loudly, thrashing, unable to be comforted, is frightening for parents. But the truth is the child is not really awake, and not even aware of her own behavior.

"Are these nightmares?" Parents will want to know how to tell them apart. Night terrors occur in the earlier part of the night, during deep sleep. Nightmares happen later on in the night and take place during REM (rapid eye movement) or light sleep. A child frightened by a nightmare will be fully awake, and if she already has language, she can convey something about what happened in the dream. Often, it can be traced to something unusual or frightening that occurred during the day. She will ask for and accept soothing and is likely to cling, afraid to go back to sleep alone. It may take her time to settle and feel reassured, but usually she will respond to reassurance, a night-light, a promise to sit by her door for awhile. Reassurance, though, will not help settle a night terror.

Night terrors seem to have more of a life of their own. Many children have one or two episodes at this age. Ordinarily, they are time-limited. But if they occur several times a night, or very frequently, or continue to occur beyond age 6, it is time to talk these over with your child's pediatrician. Night terrors are not seizures and do not indicate brain dysfunction. But they are frightening—not to the child, who remembers nothing, but to parents. It is best to let children get back to sleep without waking and without focusing on these in the morning. Leave her in the crib, or, if she's climbed out of bed, lead her back.

Handling Night Terrors

- Don't try to awaken the child.
- Leave her in her crib, or if she's climbed out, lead her back to bed if she'll let you.
- Be sure she's safe.
- Don't talk about it a lot during the day. She can't control herself, and dwelling on these episodes will endanger her feelings about herself.
- Reduce stresses on her during the day, as she may be going through a vulnerable time.

(See also *Night Terrors* in Chapter 3.)

Sleepwalking

Sleepwalking can also start in the second or third year. When sleepwalking, the child is only partly awake. A sleepwalking child can hurt herself, so you must be sure that she can't get out of the house, or into a room where there are dangers. Go to her, if you're awake, but don't try to restrain her unless you must. Instead, simply block her access to anything dangerous. Often you can gently lead her back to bed. But she may need an alarm on her door. The instructions above for night terrors also pertain to sleepwalking. Sleepwalking in children over 6 can be a symptom of being upset about something during the day. Let up on pressures that may be adding to any anxiety she is feeling. Sleepwalking can last throughout childhood as a symptom of tension, but it's not likely to if you can help the child deal with underlying pressures. Be sure she's safe! (See also *Sleepwalking* in Chapter 3.)

4 to 5 Years

Naps
During these years children who have still been taking afternoon naps will be giving them up, and parents (or teachers) will learn to get by without that precious hour or two for themselves. Most 4- and 5-year-olds still need a regular time every afternoon for quiet play, "reading," and rest. Most children this age will need about 12 hours of sleep every night, but these are also the years for new nighttime disturbances.

New Feelings, and New Fears at Night
All children this age are likely to become louder, more assertive, and to recognize that they are being more provocative. As a child becomes aware of her own aggressive feelings, she may feel overwhelmed. When she gets

away with breaking the rules, it is even more frightening. Discipline is reassuring at this age, because it says, "Someone knows where the boundaries are." Coupled with this urgent need to try out these boundaries, and the child's aggressive feelings, are the experiences that let her see whether she can get away with magical wishes. My 4-year-old granddaughter will say: "I'm in love with you. You're my Bapa and I want to marry you." "I'm already married to your grandmother." "Well, that won't matter. You have just got to do what I tell you. I'm in charge." If she heard herself, it could be pretty frightening.

These wishes and feelings can be handled during the day, but not at night. All of a sudden, a grandmother witch begins to invade her bedroom. A monster hides in the closet. Loud noises—such as barking dogs and fire sirens—take on a new meaning. Her own threats and re-taliations come back to haunt her. She senses that having these thoughts or their imaginary power is close to being out of control. Behind them is her new awareness of her limitations: "I'm really so little that I have to stomp my feet and yell." But of course she scares herself when she tries to feel powerful. She is bound to worry that the witches and monsters at night are her punishment. Children who begin to want to feel in charge are prone to nightmares as a balance to this surge in aggressive feelings. (See also *Nightmares* in Chapter 3.)

Quieting Witches and Monsters

- Emphasize the bedtime ritual all over again. Read to her. (See *Books for Children*.)
- Don't hesitate to cuddle with her, but with a limit.
- Look under the bed and in the closet. "Witches *are* scary, even though we both know they're not real."
- Comfort her when she awakens and repeat the above routine.
- Finish up the nighttime comforting with a firm ending and the expectation that she can handle it.
- Encourage her to rely on her lovey and comforting pattern as a way of handling the new threat.
- During the day, respect her aggressive bursts. Let her blow off steam. Afterward, you can even say, "That's really scary, isn't it? I get upset too when I feel angry." But make sure you set the limits she needs.
- After she's lashed out at someone, pick her up to comfort her and say, "You know I can't let you do that. It's scary, isn't it?"
- Discipline becomes even more important than ever: "I must stop you until you can stop yourself." Knowing this will give your child peace of mind not just during the day, but alone in bed at night.
- Remember that she will learn most about handling her aggressive feelings by identifying with you. When you stop yourself, let her see it. "I could have really whammed into that lady's car, but I didn't. Boy, she made me angry!"

CHAPTER 3

Sleep Problems and Solutions

Bedtime Rituals

Rare is the child who wants to give up and go to sleep—either at nap or at nighttime. The more tired he is, the more disorganized he is likely to be and the harder he will fight to stay awake. Hence, it is up to parents to set up a soothing bedtime ritual to help soften the blow. Parents can choose rituals that help the child make the difficult transition from activity and excitement to a quiet, restful state in which he can develop *his own* pattern for going to sleep.

As early as 4 months of age, begin a routine of calming a baby into a quiet state, then put him down *while he's still awake.* This way he can learn how to put himself to sleep. He will then be prepared, when he briefly wakens, to get himself back down to sleep. Otherwise, he will continue to need your help when he wakes up—at least two times in an 8-hour sleep, and three times in a 12-hour sleep. Getting himself back down to sleep is his *learned* ritual, necessary for his sleep, and for his parents' sleep. By 4 months, he is ready physically to go without a feeding for 6–8 hours. By 4 months, his brain has matured enough to be ready for his own role in learning to sleep. Helping a child learn to put himself to sleep does not mean that parents should allow the infant to "cry it out." But if he is dry and physically well, you don't need to take him out of the crib. Instead, sit beside him, pat him soothingly, and croon softly, "You can go to sleep! You can do it! You can do it yourself!" Watch for his body and breathing to begin to relax. Then, do less, so that he can learn to settle himself.

From about 9 months on, children are old enough to remember that you'd been there and to notice that now you're gone, so they may need a parent to stay in the room. Get yourself a comfortable chair—you may be there for awhile. But over time as you pat and croon less, you can move your chair farther and farther from the crib. As you gradually decrease your role in your child's sleep, he will learn to put himself to sleep.

As a child gets older, preparing for the transition to sleep begins in the early evening, after supper. No more rough-housing or wild play. (This can be hard for working parents who want *their* chance to play!) No TV or videos before bedtime. The house is quiet now. Your child will know bedtime is coming. Watch for signs that he is beginning to tire. Start your bedtime routines before he is too worn out.

A routine for each transition can be a wonderful time for communication with your baby. Gather him up to nurse him or to give him a bottle—to be finished *before* you put him down. Look out the window together and say goodnight to the darkening sky. Or carry him to his bedroom, quietly saying goodnight with him to the pictures on the wall. In a rocking chair next to his bed, rock and sing softly. Read him a beloved book. (I have read *Goodnight Moon* and *Cat in the Hat* several thousand times.)

Bedtime rituals can also be a time for passing along family rituals. As you put your child to sleep, you are bound to remember how your parents or grandparents tucked you in. Share the lullabies and stories you remember from your childhood with your child. If you don't remember them (or if you don't have positive bedtime memories), this may be an important time for you to dig up the traditional bedtime songs and stories of your culture.

Give your child a lovey—a thumb or his fingers, a soft bit of a blanket, a doll or stuffed animal, even a small part of a shirt or blouse that you are ready to part with. (Any object in the crib must be too large to swallow, but too small to cause strangulation or suffocation.) Infants under 6 months of age are more likely to use their fingers, thumbs, and hands to comfort themselves, so you may have to wait until your child is older before he really takes interest in a lovey. Teach him how to cuddle his favorite blanket or stuffed animal as a substitute for you in this transition. At the point when he is quiet and drowsy, transfer him gently to his own sleeping spot. Pat him rhythmically and gently until he subsides with his lovey. Let *him* learn his own pattern for getting into deep sleep.

As children get older, the ritual is tested. "I *need* to go to the toilet again! Just one more book! I'm scared—don't leave me!" Every possible test of limits will be used. Sometimes, the variety and number of tests show great creativity and determination. It is up to the parent to set limits on these demands. Limits are comforting, *not* hurtful. Warn him, "Two more stories and then we're through." Or, "One trip to the potty and one glass of water and that's it." Stick to it, though it may be very hard for you—especially if you've been away all day at work, or if you feel lonely yourself. Cuddling with him has been so delicious!

Bedtime Struggles

Bedtime stresses children (and many parents) with the separation that sleep brings. All children try to see whether a parent is vulnerable or not. Any excuse will do to prolong the bedtime ritual and to keep you near. By 1½ or 2 years, it becomes necessary to set reasonable, firm verbal limits. A drink of water, a trip to the bathroom, reassurance for a fear, one more story, or another hug—all may be a child's attempt to postpone the separation. When you know you are being tested, it is difficult to set limits without getting angry—unless you know from the start what your limits are, and stick to them. Since limits will be reassuring to him, set limits before you are pushed beyond yours. "Two more requests. You decide what they are! Then, lights out."

Fears of monsters and witches are bound to lead to bedtime struggles in the fourth or fifth years. They accompany the child's learning about his own aggressive feelings.

To reassure a frightened child, look around the room, in the closet, under the bed with him. "I don't see any monsters here. Do you?" Even if he says "no," you might add: "But you still seem worried. Here's your bear. You can hold him and make him feel better. I'll be right near-by. I'll leave the night-light on too, if you want me to." A night-light, a lovey, his thumb are likely to be critical—to him and to you.

Bedtime fears are to be expected. If there has been any scary experience during the day, it is probably necessary to spend extra time talking to him. The closeness at bedtime and the respect with which you handle a child's fears are important. Addressing the underlying issues with which he is grappling may be more effective in the daytime. Make a special time to be with him to just "hang out." At such a time, he may be able to unload his worries.

In addition, watch for bursts of aggression or angry feelings in the daytime. Help the child understand them, and commend him when he handles them without los-ing control. The 4- to 5-year-old period is a time, like adolescence, when feelings are likely to be out of control. Angry feelings can be frightening and costly to a sensi-tive child. Let him see how you handle your own fears and aggressive feelings. Modeling on your behavior can be a real learning experience for your child: "I felt like hitting that guy who was shouting at me, but I kept my-self under control." Don't preach, but do share. Learning to handle one's aggression is a long and sometimes painful process. Nighttime fears reflect the turmoil of beginning this process.

If nighttime fears go on over a longer period, it may be necessary to consult a mental health professional (a psychologist, social worker, or child psychiatrist) to help figure out what is behind these fears.

Bedwetting (Nocturnal Enuresis)

Overheard among 4-year-olds at preschool: "Do you wet your bed still? I don't. I'm not a baby." "No-o-o. I'm dry too." But any adult may know that one or both children are still wetting. Both are aware of the pressure, and both are trying to comply. The pressure felt by a child who bedwets can endanger his self-image very early on. By 5 or 6 years a child who still wets the bed is likely to feel like a "failure." Perhaps a parent's most important response to bedwetting is to protect the child's image of himself.

For many children, bedwetting is the most difficult hurdle of toilet training to overcome. But it also can be a problem for sleeping. Some children even try to stay awake to prevent bedwetting. Others are just not yet ready to master this major step in toilet training. But no child who wets the bed wants to. Whether they act upset or not, all will feel ashamed and guilty. Many children feel badly about bedwetting as early as age 4, even though pediatricians don't consider bedwetting a problem until age 5. I would urge that large diapers or pull-ups be an accepted part of nighttime clothing until a child says he is ready to do without them.

There are a number of reasons for bedwetting. Though usually no particular cause can be identified, it is important for any child 5 years old or older to be carefully evaluated by a pediatrician *before* trying to treat the problem. The reasons for bedwetting may differ for children who have never yet been dry at night and for those who have been dry for at least 6 months but then begin to wet again.

It is often not clear why children wet their beds. Bedwetting can run in families. If, as children, both parents wet their beds, their children are highly likely to have nocturnal enuresis, too. Children who wet their beds do not have smaller bladders. But some children with bedwetting seem to be unable to let their bladder fill completely before feeling the need to urinate.

Many children seem to sleep so soundly that they aren't roused by the signal of a full bladder. It is not clear whether bedwetting occurs during the mixed sleep–wake states that can occur at the end of the first cycle of deep non-REM (rapid eye movement) sleep. Some experts wonder if bedwetting is caused by this half-wakefulness, in the same way that night "terrors," sleepwalking, and sleep talking occur when a child awakens—incompletely—from deep sleep. As with these events, adequate sleep may help prevent bedwetting by helping the child to sleep a little less deeply and to wake up completely when he needs to.

Others now believe that children who wet the bed may not produce enough antidiuretic hormone (ADH) at nighttime to keep down the amount of urine they make. One of the medications sometimes used for bedwetting supplements this hormone, a chemical that our bodies naturally make.

Some specialists believe that stress during the second and third years—when a child is learning to control his bladder—may play a role in later bedwetting. Such stresses could include a divorce, a death, family fighting, or too much toilet training pressure on the child.

Children over 5 who have been dry for at least 6 months and then begin wetting at night are more likely to have a new medical problem, such as an infection (especially girls), diabetes, or other disorders—though most do not. Medical conditions can of course also occur in children who have never stopped wetting the bed, exacerbating and prolonging the bedwetting. Sometimes there may be a psychiatric problem, but psychiatric

To Help a Child with Bedwetting

- Protect the child's self-esteem. Whatever is done needs to be supportive, not punitive.
- You can give the child less to drink from suppertime on. Though it may not help, it can't be harmful if a child is drinking enough during the day and if you do not have to struggle with the child to enforce this.
- Two trips (low key, and NO pressure) to the bathroom at bedtime are worth a try, but don't be disappointed if they don't make a difference.
- Go with the child to the store to buy a nighttime potty.
- Paint it with glow-in-the-dark paint so that it shines in his bedroom at night.
- Put it next to his bed—to save him the trip to the bathroom. Also, it is symbolic of your wanting to help.
- If he wants you to, get him up to go to his nighttime potty before you go to bed.
- Be sure he's awake and is feeling responsible (carrying him will not encourage his own participation).
- Interrupting his sleep patterns is usually not worth it. Ensuring that he gets enough sleep, though, may help him to wake himself up to urinate when he needs to at night.
- If he wants to be successful, offer to set an alarm to go off a few hours after he falls asleep to remind him to try his potty once more. Remember, however, that he may already be wet when it does, or he may wet again later

(continued on next page)

(continued from previous page)

even if he does get up with the alarm. He will need to understand that the alarm is not meant to scare or punish him. It is a reminder that it is time for him to take charge.

- *Never* put pressure on him. *Never* make it a big affair. *Never* make it your issue. I don't like reward systems— they can mean pressure! But they are certainly better than punishment, which never helps a child stop bedwetting.
- Pressure on a child without success is more devastating than any other aspect of bedwetting. His own mastery— not yours—is the goal!

problems don't seem to cause bedwetting. On the contrary, children with bedwetting, especially as they get older, may develop emotional problems such as poor self-esteem and social withdrawal. They need a parent's acceptance and support—not punishment. Most children with bedwetting do not have emotional problems, though bedwetting is more common in children with psychiatric conditions.

If your child is 5 years old and regularly wetting the bed, whether he has just recently started or always has, start by bringing him to his pediatrician. Ask for a careful history, physical examination, and urine tests. Usually there is no need to see a urologist or mental health specialist.

Once the pediatrician has determined that there is no medical cause for the bedwetting, he or she should offer you several behavioral treatments, with the preparation, instruction, support, and follow-up you and your child need. These can include:

- Bladder control: This teaches a child to hold increasingly larger amounts of urine in his bladder during the daytime, and to develop more control over starting and stopping urination.
- Conditioning devices: An alarm or vibrator senses moisture in the sheets and goes off when the child begins to wet. This may help a child learn to rouse himself when it is time to urinate before wetting the bed. (Check with your doctor about available equipment.) Be sure that the child understands that the alarm is not meant to scare or punish, but to support him in his own efforts.
- Dry bed training: This is a difficult treatment to use because it is complicated and can involve waking a child every hour at night, in the beginning.

Although it does emphasize *positive* reinforcement, and success rates are reportedly high, this approach disrupts sleep and can easily backfire.

- Medication: For a short time (usually no more than a few months) the pediatrician may prescribe an antidiuretic hormone that may help him stay dry—especially if nothing else works. Once you know it works and is safe for your child, save it for sleepovers and overnight camp. It's best to avoid taking a medication like this for months at a time. Often when a child stops taking it, the bedwetting begins all over again.

Don't let bedwetting drag on past age 5 without seeking help from a pediatrician. Effective treatments are available, and a child's self-esteem is at risk (see *Bibliography*).

Co-sleeping: The Family Bed

For centuries, in families around the world, parents have shared beds with children. Until recently, there has been a cultural taboo in this country that made many parents feel as if it were forbidden. "You might roll over on him." As they grow older, some worry, infants might witness parents' lovemaking. On the other hand, a mother who is in favor of co-sleeping suggested, "If a child who sleeps in your bed has his own room, just use his to have sex and then return to the family bed."

Co-sleeping is on the rise in the United States. Why? Three major changes have taken hold in our society: women at work, declining buying power (the cost of living has gone up much faster than wages) for most people who work, and solo parenting.

In most families both parents work, and most parents must work more hours now to make ends meet. We think that parents are turning to co-sleeping as an adaptation to these new pressures: For many, it seems to be the only way to have time together as a family. They long to be close to their baby after they have been away at work all day. When their infant rouses every 3–4 hours, mothers who breastfeed find co-sleeping less tiring and disruptive. Separation at night seems almost impossible to contemplate for many mothers.

Single parents are even more likely to feel guilty about being away all day, and to search for a way to be close to their children when they can. (They may be lonely, too.)

Sleep problems, also, are on the rise. This may be partly due to our noisier world and more pressure on children.

But it is likely that many parents, as worn out as ever or more so, are also suffering because they haven't seen their child all day. When the child wakes up at night, many parents really aren't sure whether they want to put him back to bed or stay up and play with their child. A child is quick to pick up on a parent's uncertainty. Whatever the cause, many parents exhausted by an infant's nighttime awakenings will turn to the family bed.

By the second or third year, the child who sleeps with his family will have learned a kind of dependency on the parents' presence to help him get back down to sleep when he wakes at night. Then it will be far more difficult for him to learn to put himself to sleep, and to stay asleep through the light–deep sleep cycles.

Co-sleeping is easier and appealing for parents when the baby is little. At this point you don't need to worry about separating and pushing him to become independent. Meanwhile, the steps toward independence at night that we have outlined will soon have been missed. Then, he will be firmly entrenched in his parents' bed. Sleep is no longer his problem. His parents have become part of his sleep habits. He will not know how to get to sleep without them.

When the child is about 2 or 2½ years of age, one or both parents are likely to feel that it is time for him to become independent at night. They are tired of his constant motion, his kicking, his inability to go to bed without them. The parents blame each other: "You've made him too dependent." "Let him cry it out." They feel that the child should make the separation, and they may even be willing to let him sob his way to independence. But I would not recommend it; it is too hard on the child, and the parents. There is little that a child can learn from sobbing alone in the darkness for long periods—he has become too upset to begin the work of settling himself without a parent's help. Parents who find themselves in this position will need to make the transition step by step.

As you can see, you may not be able to teach a child to sleep independently in one night. If you let him cry it out, as some may recommend, he may finally give in, but at what cost!

Because of reports of deaths to children in adult beds, the U.S. Consumer Product Safety Commission and the Juvenile Products Manufacturers Association recommend that babies not be placed in adult beds. But the jury may be out until we know whether these deaths were actually caused by adult beds, or by other avoidable circumstances. We need an independent group to look into the questions raised by these tragic infant deaths. In the meantime, if you are concerned but want to have your baby with you in bed, see *Safety in Sleep*.

From Family Bed to Sleeping Alone—Gradually

- Reemphasize the importance of a lovey (such as a blanket or stuffed animal) during the day—for nap, going to sleep, whenever the child is stressed or injured.
- Hug him with his lovey whenever he is distressed and needs soothing.
- Use the lovey as part of the bedtime ritual. He can tuck in his stuffed animal or doll and rock it to sleep, or squeeze it against his chest (see *Bedtime Rituals*).
- Talk about how mommy and daddy need their bed and draw up a cot next to it for him and his lovey.
- Use his cot for naps and for bedtime rituals.
- Encourage him to remember a lullaby or bedtime story from your ritual together. He can try to sing himself to sleep, or to tell himself a soothing story.
- Lie down next to him until he gets attached to his "big bed."
- Encourage him to sleep in his cot, with you next to him. To begin the move from your bed to his, you may need to pull it right up alongside yours.
- When he rouses, you can pat him down, singing to him, "You're a big boy, you can do it."
- Wait for a while before you move him into his own room.
- Try to wean him to his room at naptime, and during the day.
- When you do put him in his own room, expect to go to him when he rouses.
- When he finally begins to make it alone, then you can call from your bed to him during the night.

Crib to Bed

A very common question that I hear from parents is: "When do I move my 2-year-old into a bed? I'm going to have a new baby in a month, and I'd like to give the baby his crib. Isn't he old enough for a grown-up bed?"

The answer depends on the age, size, and maturity of the child. A crib says, "This is where you sleep. You stay here through the night." When you move your child to a bed, you can no longer limit his ability to get up and explore. Don't move a child out of his crib until you have no choice—not until 3 or 4 years, if possible. But be sure to follow crib manufacturers' instructions on maximum weight limit. When your child weighs more than the crib can safely withstand, there is little choice but to make the move. Some children are just too active and will climb over the sides. Once a child can climb out of his crib, it is time to move him to a bed. Then you will be faced with how to make his room the limit—either a safety gate across the door or a bell on the door, so he can call out, but not come out. At first, you will need to go to him more often at night so he won't feel shut in.

I'd never move an older child out of a crib "just for the new baby." That's a sure way to create resentment. Either move him far enough in advance so that he's made the adjustment to the new bed, or wait—if safely possible—until afterward when he feels ready to be "grown-up" and in a "big boy's bed."

Early Morning Waking

One of our children never succeeded in getting more than 8 hours of sleep at night. She was very cooperative about going to bed at night, but she woke early and began to rock in her bed. We knew she was awake by 5 A.M., but we couldn't stand to get up with her. I often went to her to offer her a safe toy to play with. And at age 3, we encouraged her to be resourceful in her play before we came to get her.

Early morning awakening can be very difficult for parents. By 6 A.M. many children have had enough nighttime sleep (10 to 12 hours between 6 months and 6 years). If your child is waking before 6 A.M. it may be because he actually needs slightly less sleep. But surprising as it may seem, early morning awakening can also occur when a child is not getting enough sleep—too little sleep can also make it hard for a child to sleep normally. Early morning awakening may also occur when a child is getting enough sleep, but at the wrong times.

Reexamine your child's sleep patterns. How many hours of sleep is he getting at night? And during the day?

What time do his naps begin and end? What time does he go to bed at night? Does he go to sleep easily? Does he usually seem well rested when he wakes? Is he fairly good-humored and able to remain alert during most of his waking hours? The answers to these questions should help you determine whether he needs a little less sleep, a little more sleep, or the same amount of sleep, but at different times.

For the well-rested child who needs a little less sleep or who needs only a readjustment in his sleep schedule:

- Reexamine his daytime sleep.
- Consider delaying, shortening, or eliminating a morning nap if he is also napping in the afternoon.
- Be sure his nap in the afternoon does not continue after 3 P.M.
- Give him a later supper.
- Put him to bed a bit later in an effort to readjust his clock.
- Wake him before you go to bed to rock and sing to him—and to interrupt his rhythms. Many children will sleep through from 10 P.M. to 6 A.M. if you interrupt their cycle.

For the tired child whose poor sleep leads to more poor sleep, including early morning waking, you may need to lengthen naps and set earlier bedtimes. As your child catches up on his sleep, he will be better able to sleep normally—for the roughly 10–12 hours he needs at night.

All of this takes time but will not hurt the child and helps him to adjust to your rhythms. For any child who awakens too early, be sure that his room remains quiet and dark as the sun comes up and the day begins. Some children are easily roused from the light sleep of early morning by any sunlight that can get past the blinds, or by noises in the house or neighborhood. Try dark shades and curtains that fully cover the windows. He may need his windows shut, or even a white noise machine— though he may soon become dependent on the machine to sleep. If you go in to play with him when he wakes in the early morning, he'll surely wake up at the same time, or earlier, the next day—to have more time with you! Children learn early to "set their alarms" for the things they really care about.

Head Banging

Many high-strung children bang or roll their heads. Some children get up on their hands and knees and rock themselves, sometimes banging their heads on the cribsides. Very quickly, the noise becomes an important part of the comforting that rocking offers many young children. Head banging, rolling, or other rhythmic movements of their bodies are soothing to these children, as they settle for sleep, or when they wake at night, or as they move from deep to light sleep and back into deep sleep.

Head banging makes parents worry. Though it is a common pattern that often starts before a child is a year old and may last until age 3, it is hard for parents to see this behavior as the least bit comforting. But at these ages head banging is normal if a child is otherwise healthy and developing normally, and it is not to be worried about. It may last only a few weeks or months and usually diminishes within a year or so after a child first tries it out. Sometimes it seems to arise at a touch-point—when the stress of a new developmental advance such as standing or walking takes its toll. At touchpoints like these when physical activity is so preoccupying, young children may have more trouble than usual in settling themselves to sleep. Often children find other ways to comfort themselves. Sometimes, parents can help. You may be able to help your child learn to comfort himself without head banging. But even if you don't succeed, head banging in a child 3 or under is likely to stop on its own. When it is severe, it can be a sign of tension

If Head Banging Is a Concern

- First, as disturbing as it may seem, recognize that this behavior is indeed the child's way to quiet himself.
- Next, accept that a struggle with the child to give up this behavior is bound to fail and is likely to reinforce it. If you let the child know that the head banging is bothering you and that you want him to stop, you are likely to get two kinds of head banging. The head banging that he uses to soothe himself will continue, but now he's likely to add to this more head banging, when he needs your attention, or to test out his power over you! If you turn head banging into a struggle, your child will win.
- You can't expect the child to let go of his way of comforting himself unless he can replace it with another one. He may need your help to find one. Introduce a lovey (a beloved object) during the day, and encourage him to use it at night, as an alternative way for him to comfort himself.
- If he is able to move the crib by rocking, he will quickly discover that this will set up a comforting movement and sound. This racket at roughly 4-hour intervals through the night will disturb everyone. In order to keep the crib from moving, and to cut down on the noise, use rubber casters under the crib posts.
- Place the crib in the center of the room, on a thick rug that will absorb the sound.
- Offer other rhythmical substitutes that may help the child calm himself, such as music or an old-fashioned clock.

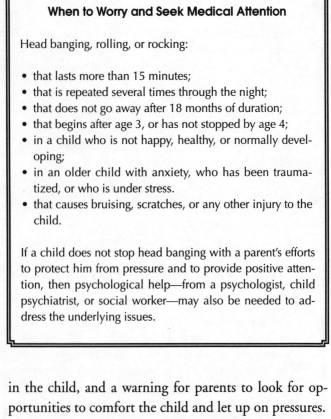

When to Worry and Seek Medical Attention

Head banging, rolling, or rocking:

- that lasts more than 15 minutes;
- that is repeated several times through the night;
- that does not go away after 18 months of duration;
- that begins after age 3, or has not stopped by age 4;
- in a child who is not happy, healthy, or normally developing;
- in an older child with anxiety, who has been traumatized, or who is under stress.
- that causes bruising, scratches, or any other injury to the child.

If a child does not stop head banging with a parent's efforts to protect him from pressure and to provide positive attention, then psychological help—from a psychologist, child psychiatrist, or social worker—may also be needed to address the underlying issues.

in the child, and a warning for parents to look for opportunities to comfort the child and let up on pressures.

Though it is frightening and disruptive for the rest of the family, head banging is usually normal in children under 3 who are otherwise healthy, happy, and developing normally. When a child has a condition such as autism, blindness, or mental retardation it is much more common. In these cases a child may actually be at risk of serious injury from head banging, and protective head-gear such as a helmet may even be necessary.

In children older than 3 who did no head banging at an earlier age, or who had stopped long ago, head banging can mean that a child is worried or stressed, or in need of your attention. Be sure to look into the stresses in his life, and in yours. Children often feel the pressure in parents' lives more intensely than parents would want. If your child needs more of your attention, try to find a regular, reliable time to share it with him—but not when he is banging his head!

Middle of the Night Awakening

Until an infant is 3 or 4 months old, he will waken roughly every 3 to 4 hours—day or night—and is bound to need a parent's soothing to get back down to sleep. After these early months, the infant will begin to be able to sleep a longer stretch at night. At 12 months, this nighttime period of continuous sleep usually lasts about 6 to 7 hours. The rest of the night, babies are likely to arouse to a lighter sleep phase, or even to wake up. When parents say that their baby is "sleeping through the night," it is likely that they are unaware of his occasional arousals and wakings. He has learned to soothe himself back to sleep—on his own. We have discussed elsewhere (see, for example, *Bedtime Rituals* and the early touchpoints of sleep in Chapter 1) ways for parents to help infants learn to comfort themselves and put themselves back to sleep. Older children may also be wakened by nightmares or bedwetting, whereas night terrors, sleepwalking, and sleep talking don't usually leave a child fully awake (see related sections). Some medical conditions, including asthma, can also interfere with sleep.

Naps

Sleep requirements vary from one child to another, and they change as the child grows. This is true for naps too. As we have seen, newborn infants will sleep and wake through the day and night. At 3 or 4 months of age, babies will need several naps during the day—totaling about 5 hours of daytime sleep. Six-month-olds usually need morning and afternoon naps. Each one usually lasts an hour or two. At a year of age, this pattern may continue though the naps may begin to shorten. Usually well before they are 2 years old, children will stop napping in the morning. They will still need their afternoon nap

To Help a Child Nap

- Strange as it may seem, a well-rested child usually has an easier time falling asleep than a tired one. Be sure that bedtimes are regular, and early enough. (See *Bedtime Rituals, Bedtime Struggles, Early Morning Waking,* and *Middle of the Night Awakening* for suggestions on improving your child's nighttime sleep.)
- Never use a nap as a threat or a punishment. Any child will certainly try to resist a nap when presented in this way.
- Prepare the child in advance for naptime. When lunch begins, remind him that naptime is coming soon. But talk about it positively, as a time to relax, read a story, and rest.
- Remove the child from all activities. Use his bedroom or a quiet place, with curtains drawn shut. If he thinks something exciting is going on at the same time somewhere else, an active child is bound to want to be there instead. TV and videos are likely to excite the child.
- Use a child's bedtime rituals—a cuddle, a story, a lullaby. Encourage him to comfort himself with his lovey or his thumb.

until at least age 3, and some children will nap until they are 5 years old.

These general guidelines should help you to know when your child's refusal to nap may mean that he no longer needs it. To be sure, you may also want to try to set up the best possible conditions for napping.

Sometimes children need help adjusting their naptimes. Whenever you are trying to change your child's sleep schedule, plan on doing so gradually. Change naptimes by only about 15 minutes (earlier or later) each day. Little by little, your child's body clock will adjust.

Infants who wake up very early in the morning and then nap later in the morning may be saving up nighttime sleep for the day. You will want to help your child stay awake for longer in the morning, pushing his nap back to a later hour. This should help him stop waking up so early.

Children between the ages of 1 and 2 may have trouble sleeping at night if they continue to nap in the morning. When this happens, it can be helpful to make the morning nap later and later, and the afternoon nap earlier. Eventually the morning nap will disappear, and the afternoon nap will be enough.

A child who has trouble falling asleep at night or who wakes up during the night may be an overtired child. This child might sleep better at night if he had a daytime nap. A child who sleeps reasonably well but won't go to bed at a reasonable time may need to nap earlier in the afternoon, or he may be ready to stop napping.

When children have outgrown their afternoon naps, they will still need some regular times in their daily rhythm to slow down. After lunch, a child who no longer naps can still benefit from a quiet time to "read" or play alone with toys such as puzzles that demand little physical activity (parents benefit too!). Although he may resist, you can talk about this rest period positively, as his time to recharge and get ready for an exciting afternoon!

Narcolepsy

Narcolepsy is a rare disorder that causes excessive sleeping, daytime napping and sleepiness, and, sometimes, short periods of weakness or even paralysis. Usually beginning during adolescence, narcolepsy can affect younger children, rarely as young as 6 or 7 years old. Children's sleep requirements vary, but also depend on their age (see Chapter One). If a child sleeps a few hours longer than the average for his age, but is not sleepy during the day, he probably just needs more sleep and both you and he are lucky. But a child who sleeps a few more hours at night longer than the average child his age, and who is also sleepy during the day, needs to be checked by a doctor. If after age 5 or 6 a child begins or continues to take naps, or if he is sleepy at school or at home, adults may think he is "slow" or "lazy." But there may be an underlying problem that needs to be evaluated.

Too much sleeping and daytime sleepiness may be caused by a variety of medical disorders, certain medications (such as antihistamines), as well as psychiatric conditions such as depression. Any child who sleeps longer than the average for his age and remains sleepy during the day deserves a careful medical evaluation. If no medical or psychiatric cause is found, a sleep study may be needed at a sleep disorders center (call your nearest children's hospital). Narcolepsy is *not* epilepsy, but it does reflect a brain condition and it can and should be treated by a specialist.

The American Narcolepsy Association (1139 Bush Street, Suite D, San Carlos, CA 94070; 415-591-7979) can also be of help.

Night "Terrors"

A frightening shriek calls you to your young child's bedroom. He may appear to be awake, yet he won't respond to your attempts to comfort him. Should you keep trying to wake him? Even if you try, he is likely to look off in the distance as if you weren't there, or he may become agitated. In fact, waking him may not be necessary or even wise. He is much more likely to settle down if you don't rouse him. After the screams subside, he is calm and has no memory of the frightening event. He'll have no leftover fears, unless his parents' fears lead him to make some up. Because night terrors are so upsetting to parents, I have tried to answer the most common questions parents ask.

Is it a bad dream?

Night terrors are not bad dreams. Dreaming occurs only during light sleep, also called REM sleep. Night terrors, however, usually occur about 2 hours after a child falls asleep, when the first cycle of deep sleep has suddenly come to an end and light waking has not fully occurred. At these times, there is no dreaming, and the brain does not form memories. During a night terror a child's heart is racing, his breathing is rapid, and he may be drenched in sweat. But he will have no dream to tell you about and no memory of his "terror."

Is it a seizure?

Night terrors are not seizures, though many parents worry that they might be. Seizures that occur during sleep are more likely to occur toward the morning, and children will sometimes wake up to feel them coming on, or remember the moments before they began. When a seizure is over, a child is likely to wake and can be soothed by a parent's comforting. Each seizure is more likely to closely resemble other seizures, whereas the behavior that goes with night terrors may be more variable: a scream, crying, babbling, scrabbling around in bed. Don't hesitate to consult your physician, though, to help you sort these out.

Is a child with night terrors possessed?

Night terrors are so surprising and upsetting that some cultures have traditionally explained these as caused by spirits or some other supernatural power. In families where such views are held, it is important for the child to know that his night "terrors" do not mean that he is "bad."

Why not wake the child?

Night terrors are not really terrors at all for the child, although they are bound to terrify parents. Any parent will want to comfort a screaming child, and will be frightened when he fails to respond. If you hear him stir or scream out, but if he appears neither fully awake nor fully asleep and looks at you blankly, stay back. He is far more likely to head straight back down to sleep if you don't talk or touch him. Your efforts to comfort him may only keep him in this strange part of his sleep, coming out of deep sleep, not fully awake, and yet unable to move on into a new phase of deep sleep. Let him return to sleep without waking him and he'll have a better night's sleep. The best protection against night terrors may actually be adequate sleep at naptime and at night.

Are night terrors dangerous?

Night terrors are common in children under 6. Because their deep sleep is often deeper than that of older children and adults, they are more likely to come up to this odd, incomplete state of waking when a deep sleep cycle ends. Night terrors are normal in this age group and are not dangerous unless a child is moving around so violently that he might hurt himself. This is rare in children under age 6 and is more likely to occur when children are older, especially during adolescence. You may need to restrain the child gently, although this may make him more agitated. It is best simply to clear away any objects that he could hurt himself with and to block his way if he heads for a window or door.

Are night terrors the same as nightmares?

Nightmares are altogether different because they occur during light sleep (REM sleep). (See *Nightmares* in the following section.)

Can night terrors lead to other problems?

Night terrors do not usually lead to other sleep disturbances—such as recurrent sleepwalking, talking, or
nightmares. Sleepwalking and talking are similar to
night terrors because they also occur at the end of a deep
sleep phase, before a child has completely awakened or
entered the next sleep phase. But they are not *caused* by
night terrors. (See sections on *Sleepwalking* and *Talking
in Sleep*.) Making too much of night terrors with the
child, at any age, may embarrass him and feel like more
pressure.

At what age do night terrors occur?
Will my child outgrow them?

Night terrors seem to be most common in children between the ages of about 18 months and 6 years old. But
between the ages of 6 and 18 months, some infants may
come up from deep sleep to a state of incomplete waking
and cry out. This is not the same as those times when infants these ages wake up and cry out for feeding, a diaper
change, or soothing. When infants wake up with a spe-
cific need, they usually respond to a parent's efforts. But
in the mixed sleep–wake state during which night terrors
can occur, infants are unresponsive to a parent's efforts
to comfort. If left undisturbed, they will eventually settle
into a light sleep.

Whether a child coming up from deep sleep into an incomplete wake state ends up rolling around in bed, screaming, talking, or walking will partly depend on his age. Toddlers are more likely to roll around in bed, or babble, until they are old enough to speak. From 2 years on screams and cries are more likely, and sometimes a child may even get out of bed to sleepwalk. After age 6, night terrors are less common, as most children no longer sleep so deeply. After 6, this mixed deep sleep–waking state is more likely to lead to sleepwalking, and emotional factors have often begun to play a role (see *Sleepwalking*).

Nightmares

Nightmares are scary dreams. They wake a child up, make him cry out, shiver, run to your bed. A child's nightmares demand comforting from a parent. All children (and adults) have nightmares at one time or another. But for children under 5 or 6, nightmares are most upsetting. Why? At 2 and 3, a child can't really understand what a dream is, or that it isn't real. How can he be sure his nightmare won't really happen to him? At 4 and 5, a child begins to understand that a dream is not real. But his understanding is still shaky. Besides, children this age still need to believe in the positive side of their "good"

dreams. So they can't yet be expected to give up their be-
lief in the "bad" ones. Even once children understand
that nightmares aren't real, they are still left to face the
frightened feelings that a nightmare stirs up.

Nightmares leave a child dreading to go back to sleep.
Sometimes, he will be unable to remember the dream,
but he can surely remember how he felt about it. He is
likely to build up a fear of going to bed if they recur often. Hence they deserve your comfort and your understanding.

Sometimes nightmares occur when the sleeping child
is uncomfortable: a numb arm that has "fallen asleep," a
full bladder, or cold feet when a blanket slips off the bed.
The annoying physical feeling seems to show up in the
nightmare as part of the scary story that "pushes" a child
(or an adult) to wake up to take care of the problem.

Nightmares are most likely to occur at times when the
child is going through a stressful period. A new baby, a
traumatic experience, a parent on a trip—all of these are
reasons for nightmares. If the stress is obvious, it is easy
to understand why nightmares are occurring and to reassure the child about them: "Of course you are worried at
night. You've been worried in the daytime ever since that
dog chased you. I'm going to sing an extra song, rock an
extra rock, and we can talk it over tonight. If you need
me, I'll come to you when you cry out for me." Your

goal is to help your child learn to conquer his fear of nightmares on his own—and he will, though perhaps not in the years when he is most vulnerable to them.

There are even more traumatic reasons for nightmares. Many young children who have experienced the death of a family member, relative, or friend will fear sleep because they may associate death with sleep. Adult explanations of death can make sleep even more frightening: "You just close your eyes and go to sleep—forever." Or, "the angels came and took him while he was asleep." Nightmares are likely to result. It can be harder to reassure a child after a death because death is so difficult for any of us to understand. Children may also remain frightened when parents are understandably sad and withdrawn themselves. But it certainly helps to provide simple, clear, and accurate information that is less likely to turn into fears and nightmares: "People die when they are very, very old, very, very sick, or when a very bad accident happens. When people die, they do not go to sleep. Their bodies just stop working—they can't think, feel, or move and their lives are over. But we will always remember the people we care about after they are dead."

There are special stages, touchpoints, in the child's development when nightmares are to be expected. Two- and 3-year-olds may have nightmares about losing their way, or being in danger without parents around to help.

Handling Nightmares

At bedtime:

- Sit down with the child to offer an unhurried time to talk about his worries. But if this talk seems to upset or over-stimulate him, it's time to stop. For some children talk about worries should be reserved for an earlier time of day.

- Accept his fearfulness and his need to hold on to you. But give him a clear signal—"five more minutes" or "one last hug"—and stick to it.

- Remind him of all of his ways of reassuring himself: songs he can sing quietly to himself, or thoughts about the fun he's had today.

- Leave a night-light on in his room.

- Encourage his lovey (such as a teddy bear, doll, or favorite blanket) as company and as a way to ward off fears.

- Try bedtime stories that help a child understand his fears and feelings—indirectly. Mercer Mayer's *There's a Monster in My Closet,* Maurice Sendak's *Where the Wild Things Are,* and Dr. Seuss's "What Was I Scared Of?" (in *The Sneetches*) are great ones to try. (See *Books for Children* at the end of this book.)

- If he comes to your bed after a nightmare, allow him to cuddle until he is comforted, and then bring him back to his own bed.

- Sit beside his bed briefly to help him make the transition, as a symbol of comfort.

(continued on next page)

During the day:

- Help him check under the bed and in the closet for ghosts and monsters, so he can reassure himself that there's nothing there.
- Help him with his "out-of-control" feelings during the day: "Remember how scared you were of the monster last night? Sometimes scary feelings in the daytime can come back as bad dreams in the night. You know when I get scared? When I get so mad I feel like hitting somebody. But I feel better when I get myself calmed down again. Does that ever happen to you?"
- Offer him simple, clear, reliable information in terms he can understand about the events in your lives that may be upsetting to him—a move, a divorce, a death. Watch his face and body language to know when you've given him more information than he needs.
- Let up on pressure when possible. Your child's nightmares may be his way of saying that he is not yet ready for the next step you are urging him to take.
- Be sure you know what television shows, movies or videos, video or computer games your child is watching. These may be violent and frightening, or they may depict adult issues that are too much for a child to understand. A child overwhelmed by information he cannot handle is bound to be a frightened child. Whether he tries to cover up his fears by acting "tough" or not, nightmares are likely to occur.

Though the "monsters" seem to be the problem, separation is the issue. The normal, healthy struggles of 4- to 6-year-olds as they try to handle their new, aggressive feelings are often accompanied by nightmares and fears. New daytime fears (about bees, or elevators, for example) or loud noises (such as thunder, fire engines, dogs barking) carry over into the night as unpredictable nightmares. A 4-year-old is likely to beg you "to look in the closet, or under the bed" for a monster or a witch. At this age, monsters and witches can represent the feelings within himself that scare him. He is learning to handle new and overstimulating feelings—of aggression, of being left alone, of losing control. Each of these deserves your understanding as he faces these feelings and learns to manage them.

Nightmares are different from night terrors. Night terrors usually occur about 2 hours after a child falls asleep, whereas nightmares occur several hours later. A child will awaken from a nightmare, frightened, and will readily tell a parent: "I'm scared." An older child will be able to say, "I had a bad dream." After a night terror, on the other hand, the screaming child will usually not wake, won't remember what happened, and won't be able to talk about it. If he does wake, he'll usually go right back to sleep. But after a nightmare, a child is likely to be afraid and may have trouble falling asleep. Night terrors usually stop after about age 6. Though children may be especially prone to nightmares at ages 4 through 6, they can occur from about age 2 through adulthood, especially at stressful times.

Safety in Sleep

At times, babies can be active during the night. They scrabble around in the bed, as though searching for a corner in which to contain themselves. A preemie researcher, Evelyn Thoman, felt that premature babies wanted to find a corner of the crib in order to wedge their heads into it—perhaps to reproduce the feeling of containment and safety of the womb that they had left too soon. As a result, a number of safety precautions are necessary to protect a baby during sleep. The following are basic measures to prevent smothering and choking. However, all parents should learn emergency measures and keep emergency numbers by each phone. (See books by Children's Hospital Boston or the American Academy of Pediatrics in *Resources for Parents* at the end of the book.) Parents should also consider obtaining training in infant CPR from their local hospital or Red Cross.

In a crib:

- It is critical that a baby's crib be stripped of any extra bedclothing that could bunch up. Infants can suffocate when their faces become wedged against or buried in a soft mattress, pillow, infant cushion, or other soft bedding. Never use a pillow in a crib.
- The mattress in a crib should be flat and firm.
- A sleeper or pajamas that fit over a baby's legs and arms can keep him warm and contained without having to use sheets or blankets that might strangle or suffocate him. Be sure pajamas and bedclothes are made out of non-toxic flame-resistant material—cotton sleepers burn in a fire.
- A soft mattress is not safe for an infant. He can sink down or burrow his head and face into it, trapping his own exhaled carbon dioxide. When this happens, the oxygen content of the air around him diminishes. He becomes dopey and won't struggle to get enough air. If an infant is co-sleeping, a parent also needs to be sure that the mattress is firm and won't sag around the baby's face and head. Don't lie too close to his face.
- Crib slats must be no wider than 2⅜ inches apart. More widely spaced slats allow a baby to fit his head between them, and possibly suffocate. Be sure

to look for the Juvenile Products Manufacturers Association certification label on both crib and mattress and on any portable crib or playpen.

- Headboards and footboards of a crib should be solid and fit snugly against the mattress so that the baby's head cannot be trapped. Cornerposts and knobs should not stick out more than 1/16 inch, to prevent strings or bedding from catching and creating a risk. Make sure drop-side latches work properly and cannot be released by a baby inside the crib. When the baby is in the crib, always keep the side rail locked in the up position.

- Be sure the crib has not been painted with lead paint or paint that flakes off. Babies will eat flakes of lead paint, which can cause lead poisoning.

- Be sure there's nothing for him to pick up and swallow in his crib. Strings or wires that hang over a crib should be kept out of a child's reach. Never use a string longer than 7 inches. Take away crib gyms and mobiles as soon as your child can push up on his hands and knees.

- Cribs should never be near radiators, windows, curtains, or other hazards.

- Sleep monitors that allow you to hear a baby cry out if he is in trouble may be comforting if you aren't nearby. But they can be overalerting. Every time the small baby moves in his bed, or comes up to light sleep, you will be alerted. As the child gets older and the risk of SIDS falls, it may help to seek the judgment of the child's doctor to decide when the sleep monitor is no longer needed.

- Crib bumpers should be firmly tied to the sides of the crib top and bottom, and at both ends and in the middle. Get rid of them once your child can pull to a stand if they are large enough to serve as a step for him to use in his attempts to climb over the railings!

- When a toddler can climb out of his crib, it is time to move him to his bed.

In an adult bed:

- If you have decided to sleep with your baby in your bed, check for potential dangers: entrapment in headboards, footboards, and bed frames (you may do best to place the mattress on the floor on a firm, padded rug in the center of the room), and suffocation or strangulation in soft bedding (these must be kept away from the infant, and off the floor around the mattress, in the event that the baby falls). If in a frame bed, help protect from falls by placing the bed on a thick, padded rug.

- Consider a co-sleeper "side-car" crib to provide protection from many of these possible dangers.
- Do not sleep with your baby if you are a heavy sleeper, or if you have taken medications, alcohol, or drugs that cause heavy sleep. These may increase the risk of rolling over onto a sleeping infant.
- Do not allow children under 6 to sleep on the top bunk of a bunk bed. Ensure that spaces between the guardrail and bed frame and all spaces in the headboards and footboards are less than 3.5 inches.

In a car:

- When your baby is sleeping in a car seat (rear-facing until 1 year and at least 20 pounds), be sure he isn't able to plop his head forward abruptly, which could possibly damage his neck muscles or his spinal cord. If your infant's head flops forward, the seat may not be reclined enough. The American Academy of Pediatrics recommends "tilting the seat back until it is reclined as close as possible to a 45-degree angle (according to manufacturer's instructions). Your seat may have a built-in recline adjuster for this purpose. If not, wedge firm padding, such as a rolled towel, under the front of the base of the seat."

- Never leave a child, especially a sleeping baby, un-attended in a car.

For more information see the Web sites for the American Academy of Pediatrics (www.aap.org) and the United States Consumer Product Safety Commission (www.cpsc.org). (See also *Crib to Bed* and *Sudden Infant Death Syndrome.*)

Sandmen and Tooth Fairies

Children old enough to wonder about the world are bound to be puzzled, and even frightened by sleep. It is a time for separation: Whether a child sleeps in his parents' bed or not, he knows that bedtime means he will soon leave their shared world for a mysterious world of dreams. Fables, folk tales, lullabies, and rituals have helped children for centuries to make this leap from one world to another. You may have grown up with your family's own stories and rituals that you are ready to pass on to your children.

Perhaps you went to sleep with stories of the Sandman. As your child dozes off, maybe he, too, can picture the same tattered old man wearily going from house to house with his bucket of sand, sprinkling a few specks on all the sleeping children's eyelids. How else did the sand get there in the morning? The Sandman can be a reliable, friendly figure for a child to count on to chase away the witches and monsters every night. By 5 or 6, children may start to feel unsatisfied by this explanation. They may feel proud of knowing this can't be true. They may enjoy testing your story out with all kinds of questions. Or they may have fun pretending along with you, wishing that fantasies could be real.

In many families in the United States, the loss of a baby tooth is celebrated as a sign of growing up. But young children are as scared of growing up as they are thrilled about it. Their fears about getting too big to have their parents nearby are bound to come out at night, when it is time to separate. Fortunately, a child who puts the lost baby tooth under his pillow can count on a visit from the tooth fairy during the night. A little less lonely as he dozes off at bedtime, he'll wake up a little richer, as the tooth fairy will exchange the tooth for a coin or a toy under his pillow. How else did it get there?

Parents use the idea of a tooth fairy to help the child feel better about the loss of a baby tooth. Even if a child of 6 is already past the stage of believing in fairies, he may insist on getting ready for the tooth fairy. He may still need to be able to believe in the dream of a magical being who looks out for him and his body!

Sleep Apnea

Apnea means that breathing stops. Sleep apnea is a frequent occurrence in children, though its significance is entirely different in infants and older children. Many older children have lapses in regular breathing at night. Though any single episode is almost always too brief to be life-threatening, they may occur over and over again each night, for months or even years. These repeated moments of labored breathing or even breathlessness interfere with sleep, and as a result can affect a child's behavior and even health. Often there is a medical cause affecting the breathing passages in the nose and throat. (See also *Snoring.*)

In infants, episodes of sleep apnea do not occur as frequently. But a single period of breathlessness can sometimes last long enough to be life-threatening and to require emergency intervention.

Sleep Apnea in Infants

Premature babies or full-term babies who have had difficult deliveries appear to be most at risk for dangerous periods when breathing stops. It may be that the brain's signals to the lungs are not yet well organized in these vulnerable infants.

In full-term infants, a pattern called "periodic breathing" is a normal development. The baby's breathing can pause for up to 10 seconds, with normal breathing in between. Parents who notice this will be worried, but it is a normal stage and soon disappears. However, if you have any concerns about your baby's breathing, never hesitate to consult your physician at once.

If your baby stops breathing for 15 seconds or more, has bluish skin, or is not moving, call for emergency help. *The Children's Hospital Guide to Your Child's Health and Development* recommends that you take the following steps:

1. Gently shake your baby's arm or leg and clap your hands gently to rouse him. He should start breathing within a second or two.

2. If he still remains unresponsive, open his mouth and look inside to make sure nothing is obstructing his breathing. Loosen any tight-fitting clothing around his neck. If your baby is still not breathing, start CPR and call 911 or Emergency Services.

When a baby has had an episode of apnea, a doctor may recommend an apnea monitor—a machine that detects periods without breathing that are too long and may be dangerous for the infant's brain. The alarm will alert parents to go in and stimulate the sleeping baby to breathe. Depending on the cause of the apnea, a doctor may recommend more observation and, in some instances, medication. (See also *Sudden Infant Death Syndrome*.)

Sleep Apnea in Older Children

Many otherwise normal children have blocked breathing passages (upper airway obstruction), often caused by enlarged tonsils and adenoids. They snore. Loudly. Breathing passages blocked by enlarged tonsils and adenoids can lead to periods of sleep apnea. As a child works to get his breath past these enlarged tonsils and adenoids, he gets exhausted.

Sometimes the tissue is enlarged owing to infection or to allergies, for example, to dust, molds, or pollen in the air around him. Snoring caused by a cold or infection should stop once the child is well again. But sometimes tonsils and adenoids stay swollen. Allergies can also cause these tissues to enlarge enough to cause snoring and occasionally enough to cause sleep apnea. Whatever the cause, if snoring persists and leads to irregular breathing or periods when breathing stops, the child should be taken to the doctor.

The doctor will check for infections. Once treated, the swollen tonsils and adenoids may shrink. But if tonsils and adenoids have been swollen for a long time, treatment of the infection may not reduce the swelling. Removing enlarged tonsils and adenoids is not necessary if they are not causing snoring and troubled breathing during sleep. But if they are, surgical removal can make a big difference. Whenever chronic snoring and sleep apnea can be treated successfully, sleep improves. The daytime behavioral problems that often go with poor sleep— drowsiness, irritability, trouble concentrating and learning, and even hyperactivity—are also likely to improve.

I have always recommended that parents clean up a child's sleeping area, removing pillows, blankets, dust on the floor that might cause a swollen, allergic reaction in his tonsils and blocked breathing passages.

Obesity can also be a cause of sleep apnea. If it is causing snoring or sleep apnea, it is time to seek help. Other causes include the shape and functioning of the throat and neck muscles, which in some children can block breathing passages when these are relaxed during sleep. Rarely, malformation of the face or mouth, or other rare disorders, can be associated with sleep apnea, though usually such disorders are obvious and have other symptoms. All deserve your doctor's attention and may need

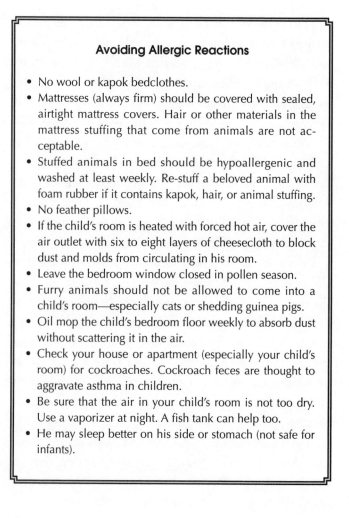

Avoiding Allergic Reactions

- No wool or kapok bedclothes.
- Mattresses (always firm) should be covered with sealed, airtight mattress covers. Hair or other materials in the mattress stuffing that come from animals are not acceptable.
- Stuffed animals in bed should be hypoallergenic and washed at least weekly. Re-stuff a beloved animal with foam rubber if it contains kapok, hair, or animal stuffing.
- No feather pillows.
- If the child's room is heated with forced hot air, cover the air outlet with six to eight layers of cheesecloth to block dust and molds from circulating in his room.
- Leave the bedroom window closed in pollen season.
- Furry animals should not be allowed to come into a child's room—especially cats or shedding guinea pigs.
- Oil mop the child's bedroom floor weekly to absorb dust without scattering it in the air.
- Check your house or apartment (especially your child's room) for cockroaches. Cockroach feces are thought to aggravate asthma in children.
- Be sure that the air in your child's room is not too dry. Use a vaporizer at night. A fish tank can help too.
- He may sleep better on his side or stomach (not safe for infants).

referral to a specialist (such as a nutritionist, sleep specialist, otolaryngologist, or pulmonologist). In rare cases, severe sleep apnea that goes untreated can even cause heart and lung problems.

Sleepwalking

Sleepwalking, like night terrors and sleep talking (see *Night "Terrors"* and *Talking in Sleep*), usually occur about 2 hours after a child has fallen asleep. Like these other mild sleep disturbances, sleepwalking often takes place at the end of the first cycle of deep non-REM (rapid eye movement) sleep, but before the child is completely awake. This strange mixed state allows the child to act as if he were awake in some ways but not in others. He can walk, even open a door, or use the bathroom. But he isn't aware of what he is doing. He can't assess the possible danger of what he is doing. He won't understand much of what is said to him and won't remember anything.

Sleepwalking is common, though less so than sleep talking. Any child who has learned to walk can start sleepwalking. It is a good reason to use a crib as long as safely possible. The crib says, "This is where you belong." Although a toddler can "cruise" along inside the crib as often as every 3–4 hours, he can't really hurt himself—as long as he can't climb out!

But as he gets older, sleepwalking can be a threat to his safety. I had an 8-year-old patient who let himself out of the house and walked out into the street in his sleep! There's not much that a parent can do about sleepwalking in a child (unless it is due to emotional stress, usually only in children 6 or over), except to be sure the child is safe, and to avoid making matters worse. Parents should take the following steps:

- Install a hallway night-light.
- Install a soft alarm bell on your child's door to alert you when he's on the roam.
- If he's in a bunk bed, switch him to the bottom bunk, of course.
- To protect a sleepwalking child from falling, his floor should not be cluttered.
- Windows should be locked if there is any chance he could open them and climb out.
- Stairways should be closed off or gated, and access to other dangers—including the front door—should be blocked.
- When your child is found walking, any attempt to restrain him may agitate him. Often, you can lead him gently back to bed. This won't interrupt his

sleep pattern. Waking him will. Waking him can also lead to embarrassment.

- Since sleepwalking and other sleep disturbances that occur during a mixed sleep–awake state are more likely to occur in older children (over 6) when they are under stress, it is important not to embarrass him or put him under more pressure, either at night or in the daytime. Embarrassing him is pressure too.

Don't talk about the sleepwalking during the day except to:

- explain to him your safety measures: the bottom bunk bed, picking up toys and other objects on his bedroom floor, the hall light, or the alarm; and
- reassure him that many children go through periods of sleepwalking and that you can make it safe for him. Most children outgrow sleepwalking.
- Be sure he gets all the sleep he needs—at naptime and at night. This may be the best protection against sleep walking.

Frequent sleepwalking in older children (usually over 6 years old) is much more likely to be a sign of psychological stress. Even if such a child's stress does not seem obvious, psychological assessment and treatment are called for.

Snoring

Occasional snoring is common in children. But 10 to 20 percent of children snore frequently. When a child snores night after night for prolonged periods, this can affect his health and well-being. Snoring is a sign of troubled breathing. This can sometimes even wake a child up, and as a result the child does not get enough sleep. (Some pediatricians believe that poor sleep can make it difficult for a child to rouse when necessary, and even think that bedwetting can result.) Fatigue, trouble concentrating, irritability, trouble learning, and even hyperactivity, impulsivity, and other behavioral problems can sometimes be caused by lack of sleep.

Snoring has several causes. A bad cold or a strep infection can cause snoring because they swell the nasal passages and throat. This kind of snoring usually goes away with the infection and should not be a cause for worry. Other causes of snoring, though, can be long-lasting. However, these causes often can be treated, and sometimes even prevented:

- Obesity: An obese child deserves help from a pediatrician, who may find a treatable medical cause for the obesity. Such a child may need a specialized team including a nutritionist and an exercise coach in order to lose weight and begin sleeping restfully again.
- Allergies causing swollen tonsils and adenoids. (See discussion of preventing allergies under *Sleep Apnea*.)
- A deviated nasal septum (a problem with the shape of the tissue that separates the nostrils, which can be repaired with surgery).
- In some children, the shape and functioning of their neck muscles do not keep breathing passages open during sleep. Sometimes, X rays, CT scans, and EKGs are helpful in identifying this problem, and treatment is available. Though their only symptoms may be snoring, poor sleep, and the daytime consequences of such, these children have neck muscles that are shaped a little differently or that relax a little too much during sleep. As a result, their breathing passages do not stay open wide enough to allow for comfortable breathing.
- Other children may snore and have trouble breathing at night if their tongues—relaxed during sleep—get in the way of their breathing passages. (There are devices that can be worn at night to help with this.)

Children with snoring that lasts beyond a cold or infection should be evaluated by a pediatrician for these causes. Some will need the help of a sleep specialist at the nearest children's hospital.

In April 2002, the American Academy of Pediatrics published guidelines for the diagnosis and management of childhood obstructive sleep apnea. All children, according to these guidelines, should be screened for snoring. (See also *Sleep Apnea*.)

Sudden Infant Death Syndrome (SIDS)

Sudden Infant Death Syndrome has long frightened parents of small infants. Also called "crib death," it can occur even in healthy-appearing infants. The peak of its occurrence is at 4 months, and by the second year it is considerably less likely. But every parent must be aware of it in infancy.

Studies of the babies who die unexpectedly have found no clear single cause. Premature infants, or infants born after very difficult deliveries, may be more likely to stop breathing suddenly. Sadly, some "sudden" infant deaths occur when babies are suffocated with a pillow by parents—sometimes desperate and overwhelmed by a child who won't stop crying, sometimes by their own struggles, such as postpartum depression, often by both. But many victims of SIDS are neither vulnerable nor abused babies.

Often it appears that a young SIDS victim may have slept in bedclothes that did not allow for easy oxygen exchange. If the mattress sags like a hammock, or if the coverings bunch up near the baby's face, he may rebreathe his own air and the level of carbon dioxide in his blood gradually rises. Above a certain level, this becomes a brain depressant. The baby becomes weak and doesn't fight to get air. He may then die from lack of oxygen to his otherwise normal brain. For this reason, an infant should sleep on a firm mattress, with no soft bedding that could move up around his face. A one-piece sleeper is preferable to blankets, and pillows do not belong in a crib. If your baby has a lovey (a beloved object), be sure it can't interfere with his breathing. If a blanket is necessary, it should be tucked tightly under the mattress and reach no further than the baby's chest.

If your baby is sleeping in your bed, the mattress should be firm, and bedclothes must be kept from entangling him. Parents need to be sure not to roll over on or too near the baby, so as not to interfere with his supply of fresh oxygen during the night. (Parents should not bring a baby into bed with them if they have taken medication, alcohol or drugs, which make them sleep more deeply.)

Since some studies have associated tobacco smoke with SIDS, babies should be kept in a smoke-free environment. Of course this is important in general for the baby's health.

Talking in Sleep

Many children come up from deep sleep to a sudden, incomplete awake state. These are also the times when children may sleepwalk or have night terrors. (See also *Night Terrors* and *Sleepwalking*.) During these times, they are confused, not fully oriented to their surroundings. Children may thrash around in bed, moan or cry out, and even say words. Parents tell me that often these are words that have just been learned, as if they are left over from the effort of learning them in the daytime. Older children too may talk during sleep, sometimes saying words, but usually gibberish.

Should you awaken the child? Why would you? If you leave him alone, he is much more likely to return into deep sleep on his own, undisturbed. If you do wake him, you may interfere with his own sleep pattern. He may be embarrassed, and tired the next day.

Since sleep talking is such a mild form of sleep disturbance, I would recommend that you let a child handle it himself. Sleep talking may occur as a sign (as other mild sleep disturbances also may) that the child is under stress or is feeling pressure. Let up on the child during the day, but don't worry about the talking at night.

As I was growing up, my elders used to say, "If you want to know what a sleep talker is saying, put his hand in a bucket of lukewarm water and he'll tell you a whole story." I've never tried it.

Teeth Grinding (Bruxism)

Some children grind their teeth at night. This appears to be more common between the ages of 3 and 7, and is increasingly less common afterward. Though sometimes harmless, the grinding can erode tooth enamel and damage permanent teeth. Some dentists will prescribe, if necessary, a protective soft mouthpiece to wear during sleep. Teeth grinding does not occur during dreams or nightmares. It is possible that it is more likely to occur at stressful periods in development and may disappear when the stress is reduced. Try offering a lovey or comforting toy and letting up on pressure. But have your child's dentist check for evidence of grinding so that his teeth can be protected if necessary.

Trouble Getting to Sleep, Staying Asleep

Trouble sleeping in a child who has already learned to sleep is often a sign of a touchpoint in development, or of anxiety and internal pressure. Sometimes there are events that have worried the child, or even traumas, from which he is recovering. Let up on all the areas that you can. If there are no traumatic events that can account for the child's worries, then I'd look for more chronic pressures. Maybe he has been feeling that he should be performing more competently. He may be feeling he's not living up to the expectations placed on him.

Trouble sleeping that lasts only briefly is often the sign of a new developmental challenge for a child: a child who is about to walk, or later, a child who is about to start first grade. But if a child continues to have sleep problems, you will need to consult his physician or a psychologist to help you and him. Sometimes sleep is disturbed by a medical problem (for example, sleep apnea or asthma), and sometimes by a psychiatric problem (for example, depression).

If a child has been frightened by a traumatic event, he may be overly sensitive to light and noise, as if still on the lookout for more trouble. Sometimes "blackout" curtains and "white noise" machines can help protect such a child from the effects of unpredictable noises and disruptions. But a traumatized child will need more help than these simple efforts to address his symptoms.

I have tried one maneuver that may help break the cycle after you have determined the reason for your child's worries. This is called self-hypnosis and can work to help an older 4- or 5-year-old to master sleep. If I know him well enough and he trusts me, I can recommend that he make up a story. The story must be his own and must be kept secret—from me and from everyone else. The story should be about something that doesn't matter to anyone, but one he can tell himself over and over. At night, after the bedtime rituals are finished and when he's comfortable in bed, he should tell himself the story over and over and over. It will gradually soothe him to sleep.

But such a solution won't work if the reason for his anxiety and the pressure on him have not let up. A parent's first job is to evaluate a child's life and see where he can be supported instead of pressured. There is now evidence suggesting that poor sleep can cause other problems—not just fatigue and trouble concentrating, but also learning and behavioral problems such as hyperactivity and poor impulse control. If the measures suggested here do not help, parents should seek professional help before the sleep problems affect other areas of the child's life.

Appendix

Bibliography

Als, H., and Brazelton, T. B. "Stages of Early Behavioral Organization," in *High Risk Infants and Children*, T. M. Field et al., Eds. New York: Academic Press, 1980, pp. 181–205.

American Academy of Pediatrics. "Clinical Practice Guidelines: Diagnosis and Management of Childhood-Obstructive Sleep Apnea Syndrome," in *Pediatrics* 109(4), 704–705 (April 2002).

Anders, T. F., and Roffwarg, H. "The Effects of Selective Interruption and Total Sleep Deprivation in the Human Newborn," in *Developmental Psychology* 6, 79 (1973).

Anders, T. F., and Weinstein, P. "Sleep and Its Disorders in Infants and Children, a Review," in *Pediatrics* 50, 312 (1972).

Azrin, N. H., Sneed T. J., and Foxx, R. M. "Dry-Bed Training: Rapid Elimination of Childhood Enuresis," in *Behavioral Research and Therapy* 12, 147 (1974).

Brazelton, T. B. "Is Enuresis Preventable?" in *Clinical Development Medicine* 48/49, 281 (1973).

Burnham, M. M., et al. "Use of Sleep Aids during the First Year of Life," in *Pediatrics* 109(4), 594–600 (April 2002).

Sadeh, A., et al. "Sleep, Neurobehavioral Functioning, and Behavior Problems in School-Age Children," in *Child Development* 73(2), 405–417 (April 2002).

Schmidt, B. D. "Nocturnal Enuresis: Finding the Treatment That Fits the Child," in *Pediatric Review* 18, 83 (1997).

Books for Parents

American Academy of Pediatrics. *Guide to Your Child's Sleep,* G. J. Cohen, Ed. New York: Villard Books, 1999.

Brazelton, T.B. *Touchpoints: Your Child's Emotional and Behavioral Development.* Cambridge: Perseus Publishing, 1991.

Brazelton, T.B., and Sparrow, J.D. *Touchpoints Three to Six: Your Child's Emotional and Behavioral Development.* Cambridge, Perseus Publishing, 2001.

Children's Hospital Boston. *The Children's Hospital Guide to Your Child's Health and Development,* A. Woolf, H. C. Shane, and M. A. Kenna, Eds. Cambridge: Perseus Publishing, 2000.

Ferber, R. *Solve Your Child's Sleep Problems.* New York: Simon & Schuster, 1988.

Sadeh, A. *Sleeping Like a Baby: A Sensitive and Sensible Approach to Solving Your Child's Sleep Problems.* New Haven: Yale University Press, 2001.

Showers, P. *Sleep Is for Everyone.* New York: Thomas Crowell, 1974.

Weissbluth, M. *Healthy Sleep Habits, Happy Child.* New York: Fawcett Books, 1999.

Books for Children

Hoban, Russell. *Bedtime for Frances*. New York: Harper & Row, 1960.

Mayer, Mercer. *There's a Monster in My Closet*. New York: Dial Press, 1968.

Osofsky, Audrey. *Dream Catchers*. New York: Orchard Books, 1992.

Sendak, Maurice. *In the Night Kitchen*. New York: Harper & Row, 1970.

_____. *Where the Wild Things Are*. New York: Harper Collins, 1988.

Dr. Seuss. *Dr. Seuss's Sleep Book*. New York: Random House, 1962.

_____. "What Was I Scared Of?" in *The Sneetches and Other Stories*. New York: Random House, 1988.

Van Allsburg, Chris. *Ben's Dream*. Boston: Houghton Mifflin, 1982.

Wise Brown, Margaret. *Goodnight Moon* (Clement Hurd, illustrator). New York: Harperfestival, 1991.

_____. *Runaway Bunny*. New York: Harper Collins, 1974.

Lullabies

Kiesler, Kate (illustrator). *Fishing for a Dream*. Boston: Houghton Mifflin, 1999 (lullabies from around the world).

Long, Sylvia. *Hush Little Baby*. New York: Chronicle Books, 1997 (a lullaby).

Resources for Parents

American Academy of Child and Adolescent Psychiatry
3615 Wisconsin Ave., NW
Washington, D.C. 20016
(202) 966-7300
www.aacap.org

American Academy of Pediatrics
P.O. Box 927
Elk Grove Village, IL 60009
(847) 434-4000
www.aap.org

American Narcolepsy Association
1139 Bush Street, Suite D
San Carlos, CA 94070
(415) 591-7979; (202) 293-3650

American SIDS Institute
2480 Windy Hill Road
Marietta, GA 30067
(800) 232-SIDS
www.sids.org

American Sleep Apnea Association
1424 K Street, NW, Suite 302
Washington, D.C. 20005
www.sleepapnea.org

American Sleep Disorders Association
6301 Bandel Road NW, Suite 101
Rochester, MN 55901
(507) 287-6006
www.asda.org

Association of Sleep Disorders Center
P.O. Box 2604
Del Mar, CA 92014
(619) 755-6556

National SIDS Resource Center
2070 Chain Bridge Road, #450
Vienna, VA 22182
(800) 505-CRIB
www.sidscenter.org

National Safe Kids Campaign
1301 Pennsylvania Ave., NW, Suite 1000
Washington, D.C. 20004
(800) 441-1888; (202) 662-0600
www.safekids.org

Sudden Infant Death Syndrome Network
P.O. Box 520
Ledyard, CT 06339
(800) 339-7042 ext. 551
www.sids-network.org

U.S. Consumer Product Safety Commission
Washington, D.C. 20207
(800) 638-2772 (consumer hotline)
www.cpsc.gov

Acknowledgments

We would like to thank Richard and Tivia Kramer and the residents of the Harlem Children's Zone for having first urged us to write this concise, accessible book on a topic of the utmost importance to parents around the country, for without their vision it might never have been written. Thanks also go to Geoffrey Canada, Marilyn Joseph, Bart and Karen Lawson, David Saltzman, and Caressa Singleton, for their unwavering support for our work, and from whom we have learned so much. As always, we would again like to thank our editor, Merloyd Lawrence, for her wisdom and guidance. Finally, we wish to express our gratitude to our families, not only for their encouragement and patience, but also for the lessons they have taught us that we have sought to impart in this book.

Index

About the Authors

T. Berry Brazelton, M.D., founder of the Child Development Unit at Children's Hospital Boston, is Clinical Professor of Pediatrics Emeritus at Harvard Medical School. His many important and popular books include the internationally best-selling *Touchpoints* and *Infants and Mothers.* A practicing pediatrician for over forty-five years, Dr. Brazelton founded and co-directs two programs at Children's Hospital: the Brazelton Institute (www.brazelton-institute.com) and the Brazelton Touchpoints Center (www.touchpoints.org), which further his work nationally and internationally. Dr. Brazelton has also created the Brazelton Foundation (www.brazeltonfoundation.org) to support child development training for healthcare and educational professionals around the world.

Joshua D. Sparrow, M.D., Assistant Professor of Psychiatry at Harvard Medical School, is Supervisor of Inpatient Psychiatry at Children's Hospital Boston and Associate Director for Training at the Brazelton Touchpoints Center. He is the co-author, with Dr. Brazelton, of *Touchpoints Three to Six, Calming Your Fussy Baby: The Brazelton Way,* and *Discipline: The Brazelton Way.*